CARDINALS RULE

TRIUMPH
BOOKS

Published by Triumph Books, Chicago.

Photography and Text by the Associated Press

Content packaged by Mojo Media, Inc.
Editor: Joe Funk
Creative Director: Jason Hinman

This book is available in quantity at special discounts for your group or organization.
For further information, contact:

Triumph Books
542 South Dearborn Street
Suite 750
Chicago, IL 60605

Chicago, Illinois 60605
Phone: (312) 939-3330
Fax: (312) 663-3557

Printed in the United States of America

contents

Reyes Reigns

Rookie Shuts Down Tigers For Series Lead

World Series Game 1 • Cardinals 7, Tigers 2
DETROIT: Rest can be overrated. The St. Louis Cardinals managed just fine in Game 1 of the World Series without much. And maybe those hard-throwing Detroit Tigers, who had a week off, aren't so tough after all.

Rookie Anthony Reyes pitched brilliantly into the ninth inning, Albert Pujols made Detroit pay for pitching to him, and Scott Rolen also homered to help St. Louis cruise past the ragged Tigers 7-2 in the World Series opener.

"Nobody expected us to win here," Pujols said. "They have a great team out there. The last thing we want to do is just show up and just embarrass ourselves."

The Cardinals have already put up more of a fight than their previous World Series, when Pujols and Rolen came up empty as Boston swept them two years ago.

With the Tigers hosting their first World Series game in 22 years, fans showed up hoping to see rookie Justin Verlander buzz through a Cardinals team that scraped its way past the New York Mets in a seven-game NL championship series that had wrapped up less than 48 hours earlier. But instead, Reyes easily outpitched Verlander in the first Game 1 matchup between rookies, taking the crowd out of it early and ending Detroit's seven-game postseason winning streak.

"We didn't play well," Tigers manager Jim Leyland said. And he made a curious decision that cost his team dearly.

First base was open when Pujols stepped to the plate with two outs in the third inning and St. Louis ahead 2-1. Chris Duncan was on second after an RBI double, but the Tigers pitched to Pujols anyway and Verlander challenged him right away with a 93 mph fastball that the slugger drove over the right-field fence for a 4-1 lead.

When Pujols came up with runners in scoring position and first base open during the regular season, he was walked in 31 of 73 plate appearances (42 percent), according to the Elias Sports Bureau. Twenty-five of the walks were intentional.

"Obviously, he burned us," Leyland said. "I'll take the heat for that."

The three-run cushion was more than enough for Reyes, who retired 17 consecutive batters before Carlos Guillen's seventh-inning single. The right-hander was lifted after Craig Monroe's homer on the first pitch of the ninth.

"I don't know if I can top this," Reyes said.

Braden Looper finished off St. Louis' first World Series victory since 1987, stopping an eight-game Series losing streak for NL teams.

Carrying only two players with World Series experi-

Anthony Reyes fires away in the first inning of Game 1 of the World Series against the Detroit Tigers.

Umpire Randy Marsh points to the plate to call Scott Rolen safe as Tigers catcher Ivan Rodriguez makes the tag in the sixth inning of Game 1. Rolen scored on an obstruction call after running into Tigers third baseman Brandon Inge while rounding third.

regular-season starts.

In fact, the Cardinals only turned to him in the opener because none of their three top pitchers was ready to go.

"He doesn't scare, he's got great composure and when he gets it rolling he's got great weapons," St. Louis manager Tony La Russa said.

Reyes had the fewest wins of any Game 1 starter in World Series history and was the first in 33 years with a losing regular-season record. He wasn't even on the Cardinals' roster for their first-round series against San Diego.

But he pitched like a poised pro.

Peering from under a starch-stiff cap and with his red-and-white socks pulled high, Reyes allowed only four hits and one walk.

"That style is not that attractive," La Russa said, referring to that hat. "I don't think it's going to be copied widely by the kids of America."

ence, the young Tigers appeared a little jittery, making wild throws and key mistakes. Detroit, which completed a four-game sweep of Oakland in the ALCS, was supposed to have the edge on the mound in Game 1. Verlander is a leading candidate for AL Rookie of the Year, while Reyes went 5-8 with a 5.06 ERA in 17

Soon after, Reyes explained his whole get-up.

"The socks I've had up since Little League, so I don't feel there's any reason to change now," he said. "But the hat helps me see a little bit, gets more light in, helps me see signs."

Reyes' performance wasn't as dominant as Bob Gibson's 17-strikeout effort for St. Louis in Game 1 of the 1968 World Series against the Tigers, but it was just as effective.

"I was just trying to be as focused as I can," Reyes said.

Rolen tied the score at 1 with a solo shot in the second, a no-doubt drive to left that proved his swing

Albert Pujols watches his two-run homer off Justin Verlander sail into the seats in the third inning of Game 1.

Anthony Reyes pitched like a seasoned veteran in Game 1.

really is coming around just as he's been saying. Playing with soreness and fatigue in his surgically repaired left shoulder, the All-Star third baseman began the night batting .188 without an RBI this postseason. His first trip to the World Series was no fun at all when he went 0-for-15 against Boston two years ago.

"It's a completely different series," Rolen said.

Yadier Molina, the home run hero in Game 7 of the NL championship series, got St. Louis going again in the third with a leadoff single. He scored on Duncan's two-out double before Pujols connected against the 23-year-old Verlander. The pitch he threw was a big mis-

take, but Verlander smiled for some reason right after Pujols teed off.

"The pitch to Duncan with two outs in the third was a pivotal point because then Albert came up and hit the home run," Verlander said. "It was a bad pitch and it was probably the biggest pitch of the night. If I made a different one, it might've been a totally different ballgame."

Verlander walked Pujols leading off the sixth, not such a good idea in that situation, and three innings too late anyway. The right-hander then threw away a pickoff attempt, and Pujols hustled to third on his ailing right hamstring.

Jim Edmonds singled to make it 5-1, and Rolen's double deep into the right-field corner chased Verlander. The rookie flashed his outstanding stuff all night, striking out eight in five-plus innings. But he also showed his inexperience, throwing too many fastballs in the middle of the plate while giving up seven runs, six earned, and six hits.

Jason Grilli relieved, and Juan Encarnacion hit a grounder that kicked up off third baseman Brandon Inge, who then threw wildly past the plate. Rolen rounded third and crashed into Inge in foul territory, tumbling to the ground in a heap. Rolen was ruled safe at the plate because of obstruction, making it 7-1, and both players appeared fine.

Inge was charged with two errors on the play.

Detroit got on the board early in its first World Series game since 1984, momentarily delighting the crowd of 42,479. Monroe, an unheralded player showing off a wealth of skills this postseason, doubled in the first inning and scored on Guillen's two-out single.

"We aren't worried. We lost the first game to the Yankees, too," Detroit's Magglio Ordonez said of the four-game, opening-round win over New York. "We just have to come back and play well tomorrow." ∎

So Taguchi singles off pitcher Todd Jones in the ninth inning, which the Cardinals won 7-2.

Rogers Cleans Up
Cardinals Bats Cool Down in Game 2 Loss

World Series Game 2 • Tigers 3, Cardinals 1

DETROIT: Kenny Rogers overcame a dispute over his smudged hand to shut down the St. Louis Cardinals and lead the Detroit Tigers to a 3-1 victory which tied the World Series at one game apiece on a chilly night. Virtually untouchable this season, Rogers blanked the Cardinals on two hits over eight shutout innings.

But what was on the left-hander's pitching hand that caused a first-inning flap? It appeared to be something dirty or dark, and umpires brought Cardinals manager Tony La Russa out to the field at the end of the first for a brief discussion. Rogers said it was a clump of dirt and resin he picked up from rubbing up baseballs. Whatever was on the Tiger pitcher's paw, it was gone when he came out for the second.

"I didn't know it was there until after the inning," he said.

In the middle of the second, Detroit manager Jim Leyland talked to three umpires near the third-base line.

"He was pretty clean the rest of the way," Leyland said.

La Russa wouldn't discuss it: "It's not important to talk about," he said tersely.

Leyland said St. Louis hitters brought the matter up.

"I know Tony said, 'Hey, I don't want to make any issue here, but a couple of my players are saying that the ball is acting a little funny,' " Leyland said. "And obviously they were a little suspicious."

Rogers extended his scoreless streak to 23 postseason innings this year and 24 1-3 postseason innings overall, a streak that began in 2003 with Minnesota. It is the longest streak since Curt Schilling tossed 25 scoreless innings in 1993 and 2001.

Rogers struck out five and walked three, improving to 3-0 in this postseason. He was 0-3 with an 8.85 ERA in the postseason before this year.

"This is where it's at and what it's all about, being able to come in here and do something like this," he said. "I've done as bad as you can do on the field. It's great to have some success."

Todd Jones came on in the ninth and allowed Scott Rolen's two-out single, then misplayed Juan Encarnacion's comebacker for an error that put runners on the corners. Jim Edmonds blooped a double down the left-field line that scored Rolen, then Jones hit Preston Wilson with a pitch, loading the bases.

After a visit from pitching coach Chuck Hernandez, Jones retired Yadier Molina on a forceout, preserving the shaky save.

Craig Monroe got the Tigers started by homering for the second straight night, a solo shot off Jeff Weaver in a two-run first, and Carlos Guillen and Sean Casey also drove in runs for Detroit. Guillen had three hits, falling a home run short of the cycle.

Rogers allowed an infield single by Rolen in the first

Jeff Weaver walks to the dugout after a rough outing in the first inning of Game 2.

that third baseman Brandon Inge could only knock down. He didn't give up another hit until Molina singled to right leading off the eighth.

In a battle of starters who failed with the New York Yankees, Weaver struggled and allowed at least two runners in every inning. He left after five, having allowed three runs and nine hits.

A night after St. Louis got the National League's first World Series win since 2003, Detroit made sure one record won't fall this year: There have never been three straight Series sweeps.

Cheating in Mr. Rogers' Neighborhood?

Say it ain't so — which is what one witness after another testified to moments after the Tigers' 41-year-old left-hander bamboozled the St. Louis Cardinals for eight innings en route to a 3-1 win that turned this into a much-livelier World Series.

When all the testimony still failed to satisfy a skeptical assembly of scribes, someone asked umpires' supervisor Steve Palermo how his crew could be certain it was nothing more than dirt — which is not considered a foreign substance under the rules of baseball — on Rogers' palm.

"This is not their first summer away from home," Palermo said with a straight face.

The funny thing is that the first inning was the only one in which Rogers had anything resembling a problem. He walked Albert Pujols with two out, yielded a single to Scott Rolen, ended it by enticing Juan Encarnacion into grounding back to the mound and set down the next nine Cardinals he faced.

Rogers had never lasted beyond the fifth in all five of his previous postseason starts. But since arriving in Detroit this year, and making all three of his playoff starts at home, he's done a fair imitation of Christy Mathewson. In fact, Mathewson's record of 27 scoreless

innings is now just four innings from Rogers' grasp.

"I'm no Christy Mathewson, that's for sure," Rogers said with a chuckle, "but I've had scoreless streaks before."

None quite like this one, though.

Let's assume -- at least for the moment -- that the verdict in "Smudgegate" is the right one. Either way, it left a lot of people scrambling to explain how Rogers -- his denial aside -- reinvented himself as the ghost of Mathewson of postseasons past. He cited maturity, and the knowledge that a pitcher his age gets fewer and fewer chances to shape his legacy.

"If you worry about failure, it's coming. And sometimes, you get caught up in that as an athlete," Rogers said. "I'm focusing on every pitch, every hitter, I'm not looking past an out or an inning."

Leyland, though, was much more specific. He zeroed in on a chance to get even with the team that lured Rogers to New York with a fat contract and the demanding fans that ran him out of town too quickly afterward.

"I think probably the big thing was the Yankee game," the manager said, referring to Rogers' sterling 7 2/3 innings against New York in Game 3 of the division series, the performance that launched the left-hander's postseason streak.

"I think he was so pumped up to pitch against the Yankees, he had some past experience there, some history, most of it good and I guess, some not so good. For whatever reason, that Yankee series got him pumped up like I've never seen a pitcher.

"In fact," Leyland said, "it makes me nervous to see someone that pumped up."

If so, considering Leyland's smoking habit, Rogers' shaky first inning must have required at least three cigarettes. The Gambler came out steaming on a night when the game-time temperature was 44 degrees and teammate Placido Polanco, who was wearing a hooded

Kenny Rogers, who was caught with a foreign substance on his hand early in the game and was asked to wash it off, winds up in the seventh inning of Game 2.

Carlos Guillen watches an RBI double in the first inning of Game 2. Looking on are Yadier Molina and home plate umpire Alfonso Marquez.

and piling them on through a 99-pitch evening.

The pitches that everybody talked about afterward, though, were the 18 that Rogers threw in the first inning with that smudge still on his hand. Since baseball began, pitchers have scuffed baseballs with belt buckles, wedding rings and emery boards, slathered them with spit, Vaseline, shaving cream and hair gel -- or pretended to as a way to put hitters off-balance.

"If it distracts someone," Rogers said, "I'd do anything to distract anybody. But I think after the first inning, it was fine. I don't think anybody had a prob-lem with anything."

After the first inning, no.

But someone in the St. Louis clubhouse watching the telecast saw what the rest of the nation did -- Fox showed a closeup of the smudge -- then passed word to the dugout. That set the cleanup in motion and presumably put the Cardinals' fear to rest.

Asked afterward whether he believed Rogers had deliberately put anything on the ball, Cardinals second baseman Aaron Miles said simply, "No."

But a second later, he curiously added, "Pine tar is a funny thing. You can give somebody a high-five after he hits a home run and if he's got it on his hand, you'll have it on your hand." ∎

undershirt beneath his cap, looked like he was dressed to go snowmobiling. The pitcher pumped his fist with every inning-ending out and seemed to be choreographing his outfielders' movements every time they took off in pursuit of a Cardinal fly ball.

But Leyland had the adrenaline business right. The more Rogers got worked up, the faster he started throwing. His breaking ball was on much of the night, but he kept pushing the radar gun higher with fastballs, cracking the 90-mph barrier in the sixth inning

David Eckstein soars over Ramon Santiago in the second inning of Game 2 to turn a double play.

Carpenter Nails Down Game 3
Ace Sends Tigers Down Quietly

World Series Game 3 • Cardinals 5, Tigers 0

ST. LOUIS: Chris Carpenter presented his right hand for inspection. The manager and umpire looked, and everyone was satisfied. The St. Louis ace had a cramp, that's all, and he stayed on the mound. He'd waited a long time to make this start and clearly nothing was going to blemish this outing.

Carpenter kept the Detroit Tigers in their hitting funk and put the World Series focus back on the field, pitching the Cardinals to a 5-0 victory for a 2-1 edge.

"He's so strong between the ears that nothing fazes him," Cardinals manager Tony La Russa said. "He's got a good head, good heart, good guts."

Gone were any reminders of the squabbling, accusations and denials Kenny Rogers caused with his smudged left hand in Game 2. Oh, Rogers heard plenty from the sellout crowd at Busch Stadium during pregame introductions, as chants of "Cheat-er!" echoed throughout the ballpark. But that was about the only noise the Tigers caused in this game.

Staring at catcher Yadier Molina's mitt, Carpenter's concentration was unshakable.

"Go one pitch at a time," Carpenter said. "All that stuff around you that's going on doesn't get in your head, so you're not even thinking about it."

Carpenter threw big curves to spin three-hit ball for eight innings. Jim Edmonds delivered a two-run double and St. Louis took advantage of sloppy play to score its three other runs. Pitching usually rules the postseason, and that's been the case so far. The Cardinals hope to present even more in Game 4 Wednesday night when NL championship series MVP Jeff Suppan starts against Jeremy Bonderman.

The Tigers' trio of leadoff man Curtis Granderson, ALCS MVP Placido Polanco and postseason veteran Ivan Rodriguez is combined 0-for-34 after three games. Manager Jim Leyland said he's considering lineup changes.

"They'll get going," Tigers teammate Sean Casey said. "I think it takes that one hit to get that confidence and it'll probably snowball from there."

Carpenter showed why he won the NL Cy Young Award last year and is a top contender this season. He struck out six, walked none and permitted only one runner past first base. Carpenter's lone problem came in the seventh inning. As Polanco led off by lining out to good friend Albert Pujols, Carpenter hopped off the mound and looked at his hand.

La Russa, a trainer and the entire St. Louis infield converged on the mound, studying Carpenter's pitch-

Albert Pujols celebrates after a fourth inning double off Detroit Tigers pitcher Nate Robertson in Game 3.

Cardinals Rule

Jim Edmonds swats a bases-loaded double to drive in two runs against pitcher Nate Robertson in Game 3.

ing hand. Plate umpire Wally Bell also went out to check as reliever Josh Kinney began warming up.

The problem: Jammed when he batted in the fourth inning, his hand was a bit balky.

"It felt kind of funny from that point on," Carpenter said.

"They think I might have just bruised it in there or something like that," he said. "We'll deal with it tonight, but I think it will be fine."

He certainly drew a lot more attention than Rogers attracted after a yellowish-brown mark was spotted on his hand--he said it was a mix of dirt, spit and resin, while others claimed it was illegal pine tar.

Carpenter drew his biggest roar when he got a standing ovation as he came to bat in the eighth. The bottom of the eighth took a while, though, and Braden Looper relieved in the ninth and finished the combined three-hitter.

"We need to swing the bats better, obviously,"

Leyland said.

The Tigers had homered in all 10 postseason games before Carpenter stopped them. A Detroit team that averaged 5 1/2 runs per game throughout the AL play-offs has scored a total of five in the World Series.

It was somewhat of a surprise, too. Carpenter gave up a season-high seven runs at Detroit in June, and the Tigers' starting lineup was hitting .356 against him.

"We faced him before and hit him pretty good, but tonight he pitched great," said Detroit's Carlos Guillen, who was hitting .714 before going 0-for-3. "He's a Cy Young winner."

Carpenter had waited a long time for this opportunity. He was injured and missed the entire 2004 postseason, including the Cardinals' matchup with Boston in the World Series, a Red Sox sweep.

Carpenter beat San Diego twice in the first round of this year's playoffs, but struggled twice against the New York Mets in the NLCS at Shea Stadium. Back at Busch, where his ERA is doubly as good as it is on the road, he was in complete control on a chilly evening.

Edmonds hit his go-ahead double in the fourth. A throwing error by Tigers reliever Joel Zumaya gave St. Louis two runs in the seventh and a wild pitch by Zach Miner let another run score in the eighth.

Working on 13 days' rest, Tigers lefty Nate Robertson opened with three hitless innings. That's about normal for the Cardinals -- they were a weak 23-34 against left-handed starters this season.

Yet it was the lefty-swinging Edmonds who got the key hit against Robertson, who was pulled after five innings. After that, Robertson bided his time on the bench talking to Rogers, perhaps picking up some secrets about pitching in cold weather.

"It's almost like what Kenny did in Game 2, Chris Carpenter did tonight," Casey said. "He was pretty much lights out." ∎

Preston Wilson is forced out at home by Ivan Rodriguez in the fourth inning of Game 3.

Eckstein Stands Tall
Diminutive Shortstop Leads Comeback

World Series Game 4 • Cardinals 5, Tigers 4

ST. LOUIS: Judging from statistics, logic and just about anyone you ask, the Cardinals had no business even being in this World Series. They have only one hitter who can scare a team — and he hasn't been hitting.

"We don't really go by what people say," said that one batter, Albert Pujols. "We know the talent in this clubhouse."

They also know that they are one win away from being one of the most improbable world champions ever. Because of a third double (and fourth hit) on the night by the 5-7, 165-pound David Eckstein, as improbable a big-leaguer as you'll see, the Cardinals, having won only 83 games this regular season, won Game 4, 5-4.

They took a 3-1 lead in the Series and, naturally, they did it improbably. Speaking of Eckstein, Cardinals manager Tony La Russa said, "He's the definition of a clutch player. He's the toughest guy I've ever seen in a uniform."

It is not every day that a team ties a game after the opponent's sure-handed and fleet-footed centerfielder slips while chasing a routine fly ball, but that's what happened in the game-turning seventh inning. Curtis Granderson lost his footing on a field that was wet after a rainout Wednesday (but that is known to drain well), and Eckstein reached second.

"We had an unfortunate break on a ball in the outfield," Tigers manager Jim Leyland said. "It's all part of it."

Yes, he remembered Curt Flood of the Cardinals stumbling and failing to catch a fly in Game 7 against the Tigers in 1968: "But right now, I'm not really interested in Curt Flood."

Eckstein scored the tying run when reliever Fernando Rodney's throw to first on a sacrifice attempt sailed high and down the rightfield line. A Detroit pitcher has committed an error in each of the four games. With two outs, Preston Wilson, a player who was so bad early this season that he was released by the weak-hitting Astros, grounded a tiebreaking single to left.

"Yes, I'm proud he's here," said his stepdad, Mookie Wilson, who knows something about grounders and the World Series.

Logic did make a comeback in the eighth when former Met Braden Looper blew the lead. He allowed a double to the previously slumping Ivan Rodriguez (his third hit of the night) and Brandon Inge tied it with a double off closer Adam Wainwright.

But in the bottom of the inning, a walk, a forceout and a wild pitch on a strikeout put a runner on second for Eckstein, who looks more like a vendor than a big-leaguer. He doubled off the glove of diving leftfielder Craig Monroe and the Cardinals had their most important lead of this odd season.

David Eckstein doubles to center to drive in a run in the eighth inning of Game 4 as the Cards went on to beat the Tigers 5-4.

Adam Wainwright celebrates after retiring the side in Game 4.

that span as the Mets had in two games against him in the NLCS. Sean Casey had two of them, a home run to right in the second to make it 1-0 and a two-out single to center in the third that drove in Granderson (who doubled) for a 2-0 lead. Then Rodriguez got his second hit, a run-scoring single to right.

Leyland had been just as emphatic in his faith in starter Jeremy Bonderman as in his lineup. Because of the rainout Wednesday, he could have skipped back to Game 1 starter Justin Verlander but was adamant about going with all four of his regulars.

Bonderman did cause the Tigers to hold their breath. He gave back one run in the third on Eckstein's double and another in the fourth on doubles by Scott Rolen and Yadier Molina. Bonderman left his club in a sticky spot: men on first and third with one out in the sixth of a 3-2 game. But Rodney smoothed that out by striking out Aaron Miles and pinch hitter John Rodriguez.

Now the Tigers have to be perfect.

"Can we do it? Absolutely," Leyland said. "Are we in good shape? Absolutely not."

But they are up against an imperfect club that has become hot at the perfect time.

"We went through a lot of issues this year. The most consistent thing we had this year was heart," La Russa said, adding that he had his starting lineup intact for the postseason. "When we put that team out there, we're a pretty good team." ■

"I was just hoping to find a way to put the barrel of the bat on the ball," said Eckstein, who had been called "the All-American baseball player" by Leyland. "It's nice to actually have a little luck involved."

The Tigers jumped ahead 3-0 by the third inning, collecting as many hits (five) against Jeff Suppan in

Jeff Suppan pitches to Curtis Granderson in the first inning of Game 4.

Red Hot!
Cardinals Win 10th World Championship

World Series Game 5 • Cardinals 4, Tigers 2

ST. LOUIS: Favored by few, the St. Louis Cardinals used an unlikely cast of characters to win their first World Series in nearly a quarter century.

Jeff Weaver dominated, David Eckstein drove in two runs on balls that didn't leave the infield and the Cards took advantage of another wild throw by a Tigers pitcher to beat Detroit 4-2 and won the Series in five games.

"I think we shocked the world," Cardinals center fielder Jim Edmonds said. "It's an unbelievable experience."

Manager Tony La Russa's Cardinals had just 83 regular-season wins, the fewest by a World Series winner, and nearly missed the playoffs after a late-season slump. But the Cardinals beat San Diego and the New York Mets in the playoffs, then won their first title since 1982 by taming a heavily favored Tigers team that entered the Series with six days' rest.

After closer Adam Wainwright struck out Brandon Inge for the final out, the ballpark erupted. Wainwright raised his arms in triumph, catcher Yadier Molina ran to the mound and the pair bounced off toward second base, where they were joined by teammates running out from the dugout and the bullpen.

"I don't think anybody in uniform didn't do something in the postseason. Everyone did," said La Russa, whose uniform number – 10 – now matches the team's World Series titles. "The defense was great. The pitching was great. Timely hitting. The best bench I've had in a long time. They just refused for us to lose."

Minutes later fireworks filled the sky above the ballpark.

Eckstein, the 5-foot-7 shortstop who had four hits in Game 4, was the Series MVP.

"No one believed in us, but we believed in ourselves," Eckstein said.

On a cold Midwest night more suitable to football than baseball, the Tigers made two more errors, raising their Series total to eight – three by Inge, the third baseman, and a record five by their pitchers. Eight of the 22 runs allowed by the Tigers were unearned, the most by a team since the 1956 New York Yankees against Brooklyn.

While the Tigers tossed the ball to the tarp, the Cardinals were mostly crisp, with the notable exception of right fielder Chris Duncan, who dropped a fly ball just before Sean Casey's two-run homer in the fourth put Detroit ahead 2-1.

St. Louis came right back to take a 3-2 lead in the bottom half as pitcher Justin Verlander threw away a ball for the second time in two starts, and Scott Rolen added a big run with a two-out RBI single in the seventh off reliever Fernando Rodney, extending his post-

Adam Wainwright celebrates with catcher Yadier Molina as the Tigers' Sean Casey walks off the field in the ninth inning of Game 5.

David Eckstein holds the World Series MVP trophy after the Cardinals beat the Tigers 4-2 to win the 2006 World Series in five games.

season hitting streak to 10 games.

It was the Cardinals' first title since 1982 and the first for the NL since the 2003 Florida Marlins. La Russa, who led the Oakland Athletics to a sweep in the earthquake-interrupted 1989 Bay Bridge Series, joined Sparky Anderson (Cincinnati and Detroit) as the only managers to win Series titles in each league.

It marked the first time since the 1912 Red Sox at Boston's Fenway Park that a team won the Series at home in a first-year ballpark. And the Cardinals (83-78) almost didn't even make it to the postseason. They had a seven-game NL Central lead with 12 to go but lost eight of nine before recovering to finish 11/2 games ahead of Houston, the defending NL champion.

Minnesota, in 1987, had set the previous low for wins by a Series winner, going 85-77.

"The team that wins a world championship is the team that played the best," La Russa said.

As the Tigers failed in their bid for their first title since 1984, their season ended with Kenny Rogers rested and ready with no place to pitch. Rogers, who threw 23 shutout innings in the postseason, was saved by manager Jim Leyland for a possible sixth game Saturday in Detroit.

Weaver, cast off by the Yankees three years ago after a World Series flop, allowed four hits in eight innings, matched his season high with nine strikeouts and walked one before Wainwright finished for the save. St. Louis pitchers held Detroit to a .205 average (33-for-161) over the five games.

Verlander gave up three runs — one earned — and three hits, recovering from early control problems to give the Tigers a decent effort.

After a daylong rain, the weather cleared about two hours before gametime. Still, it was 47 degrees when play began, and a brisk wind made it feel that much colder. But the wintry conditions didn't dampen the enthusiasm of the 46,638 mostly red-clad fans.

Verlander, throwing up to 100 mph, was wild in the first inning, walking the bases loaded and throwing two wild pitches. By his fourth batter, Jason Grilli was warming up in the bullpen, but Verlander escaped by the thinnest of margins, needing 35 pitches to get through the inning.

He walked Duncan with one out, threw a wild pitch, then walked Albert Pujols. With a 2-0 count on

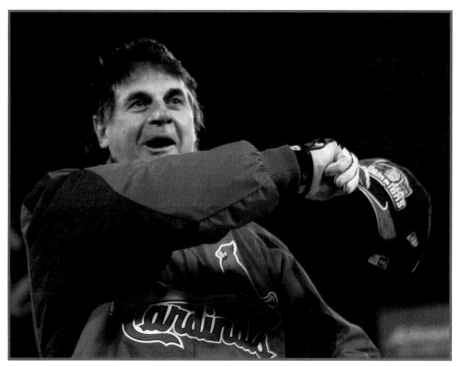

Tony La Russa waves to fans just a moment before accepting the 2006 World Series trophy.

his bat headed toward third. Inge dived and grabbed the ball as it went over the base and then, even though he had plenty of time, rushed his throw. It bounced and went up the line as Molina scored. Eckstein was given a hit on the play and advanced on the bad throw by Inge.

Weaver held the Tigers to two hits in the first three innings. With one out in the fourth, Magglio Ordonez lofted a fly to right and Duncan, calling off center fielder Edmonds, allowed it to kick off his glove for a two-base error.

Casey sent the next pitch into the seats down the right-field line for a two-run homer that put Detroit ahead. Then it was the Tigers' turn to make a key mistake.

Molina and Taguchi singled with one out in the bottom half and Weaver bunted back to Verlander. He had an easy force at third, but sidearmed the ball and it bounced past Inge for an error that allowed Molina to score the tying run and left runners on second and third.

Eckstein followed with a grounder to shortstop that drove in Taguchi for a 3-2 lead. Duncan had another adventure in the fifth, letting Casey's catchable two-out fly drop behind him on the warning track for a double. But Weaver struck out Rodriguez on a checked swing.

Pujols turned in the niftiest play, sprawling to snare Placido Polanco's grounder to first leading off the seventh, then making a one-bounce throw from his back to Weaver covering the base. ∎

Edmonds, pitching coach Chuck Hernandez came to the mound. Edmonds fell behind 3-0, then flied out after Verlander worked the count full. Following another wild pitch, Verlander walked Rolen, and when he started Ronnie Belliard with a ball, catcher Ivan Rodriguez went to the mound.

After fouling off a 3-2 pitch, Belliard hit a grounder up the middle that Carlos Guillen just got to in time to make an off-balance throw to first, beating Belliard by less than a step as Casey scooped the ball on a bounce. Verlander yelled and whipped his arm across his body excitement.

But St. Louis went ahead in the second, after Molina looped a single to center leading off, took second on So Taguchi's bunt and third on Weaver's groundout. Eckstein hit a smash, and both the ball and a chunk of

Good Intentions

Tigers Elect to Pitch to Pujols, and Pay the Price

DETROIT: Albert Pujols showed up at the World Series hitting what baseball people like to call a "quiet" .324.

That made it sound as if the St. Louis slugger walked all the way to Motown on his tippy-toes, but no. In this case, quiet meant Pujols was putting up respectable numbers in the postseason boxscores, but not enough, finally, on the scoreboard. Not enough, anyway, for a guy widely regarded as the most dangerous hitter in the game.

That all changed with one swing of the bat in Game 1 of the World Series.

Pujols re-directed the first pitch he saw in the third inning—a 94 mph fastball from hard-throwing Detroit starter Justin Verlander—into the right-field seats for a two-run homer and the road-weary Cardinals went on to steal a 7-2 decision.

That one swing also ignited a debate that will rage for the rest of this Series: Pitch to Pujols? Or not?

"I could go into a lot of detail about that," Tigers manager Jim Leyland said tersely, "but I'll leave it at this: The manager's decision is either to pitch to him or walk him. I pitched to him and obviously he burned us.

"I'm not going to get into a lot of explanation about what the thinking was. But I take the bullet there and if somebody gives criticism you accept it, because it's ultimately my decision."

Leyland is an old-school manager who hates giving anybody anything for free, which means every Pujols' at-bat from here on out is likely to turn into a chess match. Leyland has considered giving up smoking more times this season than giving a hitter—any hitter—an intentional walk. So it's a safe bet that every time the camera catches him during one, expect to see a lighted cigarette dangling from his lips.

The Tigers issued just 35 free passes during the regular season, the sixth-lowest total in the American League. Before Game 1, the only time Leyland saw Pujols up close and personal was during a three-game series against St. Louis in June, and he walked him intentionally exactly once.

And before this one, Leyland was very cagey about his plans. But Verlander went right at Pujols in the first inning, mixing fastballs and curves, snapping off a sharp breaking ball at 2-2 and striking him out. Then came Pujols' first swing in the third, and it quickly made any debate about strategy irrelevant.

"I just try to see the ball," Pujols explained, "and put a good swing on it."

Verlander went back to the same mix in the sixth, tickling the radar gun at 76 mph with a curve and pushing it to 95 on the next with another fastball. His final pitch of the sequence, at 3-2, was another one of those fall-off-the-table breaking balls, but it fell just far enough off the plate to walk Pujols.

The St. Louis Cardinals' Incredible 2006 Championship Season

Pujols hits into a fielder's choice off Detroit Tigers pitcher Joel Zumaya during the seventh inning in Game 3 of the World Series. Zumaya's subsequent throwing error allowed the Cardinals to score two runs.

Pujols attempts to throw out Sean Casey at third base on a bunt single by Ramon Santiago during the fourth inning in Game 2 of the World Series.

"If I've got an arm like Verlander, what do you do the first time you face him? What do you do the next time?" Cardinals manager Tony LaRussa said, glad he didn't have to answer either question. "He walked him.

"But the guy behind him got two hits tonight. And Jim is very aware of that—in fact, both of guys behind him got two hits. That's part of our strength.

"Albert is very dangerous, but these two guys, when they're swinging, and they're swinging well, be careful putting them on base," La Russa added, "because it will lead to runs, I think."

On that particular night, that was more than a hunch.

After Pujols walked, Verlander tried picking him off and his throw bounced away from first baseman Carlos Guillen and rattled around the right-field wall with several Tigers in pursuit. Even with a hamstring injury that limited his effectiveness against both the Padres and Mets, Pujols motored all the way to third.

His pained expression made it clear that running is still an effort, but at least the pain didn't last long. Jim Edmonds drilled a single to right, allowing him to stroll leisurely home with St. Louis' fifth run. Then Scott Rolen doubled behind Edmonds and the chain-reaction was complete. Just don't forget who started it.

"I don't want to put any pressure on myself," Pujols said, "because I have a lot of guys that can help the

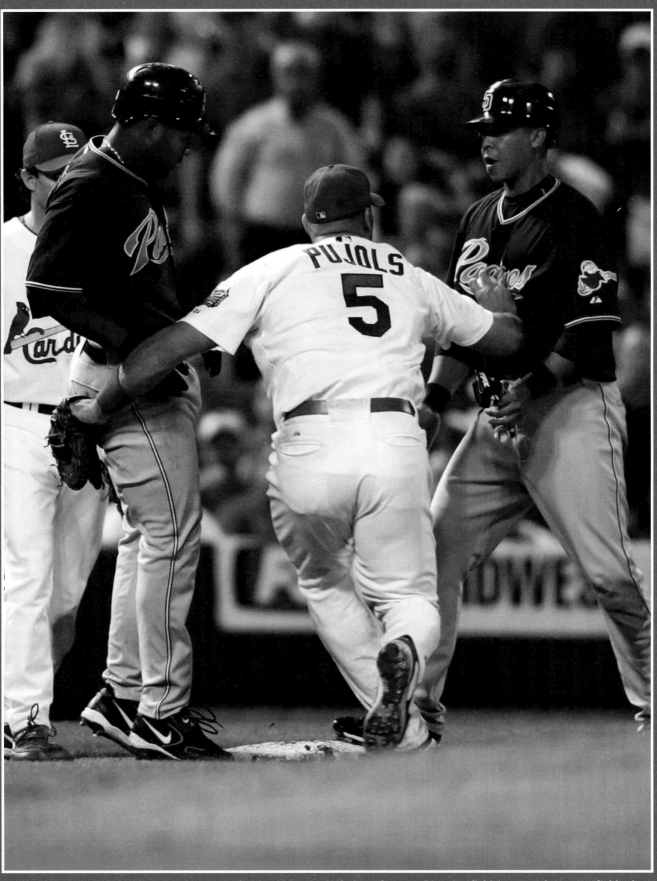

Pujols tags both San Diego Padres' Josh Barfield and Terrmel Sledge after catching Barfield in a rundown. Barfield, the lead runner, was out on the play as Sledge had already advanced to third

Pujols hits a ground rule double off Detroit Tigers pitcher Nate Robertson in the fourth inning of Game 3 of the World Series.

Pujols shatters his bat as he grounds out to third during the sixth inning in Game 3 of the NLCS.

team a lot of different ways."

But not enough did before the World Series. Edmonds was hot at the start of the postseason, getting three hits in his first seven at-bats, but had gone .214 since. Rolen, struggling with a bad shoulder, came in at .188.

In the NL division series, the Padres weren't scared enough of either to walk Pujols, intentionally or otherwise, and issued him just one base on balls in four games. He responded by driving in three runs.

The Mets took a different tack in the NLCS, walking him intentionally four times, and seven in all in seven games. Pujols collected one RBI, but it was a

Game 5 homer off Tom Glavine that launched St. Louis' comeback.

The truth is that there's no right answer. The Elias Sports Bureau found that during the regular season, when Pujols came up with runners in scoring position and first base open, he was walked 42 percent of the time. Of the 31 times he did walk, 25 were intentional.

Considering Pujols' final regular season numbers—.331, 49 home runs and 137 RBIs—deciding whether to pitch to him is like choosing between water torture or a cigarette and a blindfold. Whichever Leyland chooses, Pujols will be ready.

"You can't get caught up worrying, 'Is he going to pitch to me?' You've just got to go up like you do every time," Pujols said. ∎

Albert Pujols and Yadier Molina celebrate after the Cardinals beat the Tigers 7-2 in Game 1 of the World Series.

A Late, Great Bloomer

Cardinals' Carpenter Getting Better with Age

ST. LOUIS: At the same house and in the same room where he told his wife he was ready to give up baseball, Cardinals pitcher Chris Carpenter got the call that confirmed why she refused to let him.

His newborn daughter was hungry, his toddler son was yelling, and that's when Carpenter learned he'd made history two seasons after being ready to send his career into it.

His comeback now included the 2005 Cy Young Award.

Carpenter's son, Sam, did a little dance to celebrate.

Alyson Carpenter, who talked her husband back into baseball, hugged him.

"It's one of those memories that will always stick in my head—we sat here until about 3 in the morning crying and talking about my career," Carpenter said from his home in New Hampshire, describing what happened there late one night in July 2003. "I was ready to be done. She didn't think I was done. And that I would regret it if I didn't take that one more step and try to come back.

"I know that if it wasn't for her I wouldn't be here."

Willis had more wins than any other pitcher in baseball in 2005 (22), and Carpenter is the only pitcher in the live-ball era to go undefeated over 16 consecutive starts while pitching at least seven innings in each start and never allowing more than three earned runs. That was the core of the run in which Carpenter had 22 consecutive quality starts, the longest streak in the league since Bob Gibson's 22 in 1968.

Gibson was the last Cardinal to win the Cy Young, doing so in 1970, and the only other Cardinal to win the Cy Young, having also won in 1968.

In 2004, Carpenter went 15-5 and won the comeback player of the year award from his peers. But he missed the postseason with a biceps injury. General manager Walt Jocketty said he recalled pitching coach Dave Duncan remark in spring training that year that Carpenter's focus hinted at luminous possibilities.

Around Jupiter, Fla., there were whispers of the righty being Cy Young-caliber.

This was less than 19 months after he was ready to quit.

In 1999, Carpenter was the young turk on a Toronto pitching staff that featured two Cy Young winners (Clemens and Pat Hentgen) and two future Cy Young winners (he and Roy Halladay). His future was bright; people told him so. In 2002, he was named the Blue Jays' opening day starter. Four days later, he made the first of three visits to the disabled list that season.

By the end of it, he had shoulder surgery and was a free agent. He signed with the Cardinals, made a total of eight minor league appearances in 2003 and still felt pain in his pitching arm. He returned home in July,

Chris Carpenter has been a dominant pitcher the last few years, but if it wasn't for his wife's encouragement, he might have already retired.

Carpenter reacts after a double play to end the seventh inning against the Tigers in Game 3 of the World Series.

after he "couldn't even play catch" following a Class AA start.

"I was (tired) of going to work hurting every day," Carpenter said. "I was not thinking 100 percent clearly about what I wanted to do. I was to the point where I didn't want to do it anymore. I'll go get a regular job, whatever it is I didn't know.

"I was ready to go. Fortunately, (Alyson) wasn't."

A second surgery to his shoulder, this one by Cardinals team doctors, mended the pain and

Carpenter embarked on his comeback year the next spring. There was much more to his return than health, however. Carpenter admitted that he "gave a lot of games away in Toronto because I wasn't 100 percent prepared. There were definitely games that mentally I wasn't there like I needed to be."

The lessons learned from Clemens and Hentgen took root during his recovery, and he plunged into Duncan's philosophy of pitching, becoming buzzsaw focused, giving no game, no inning away.

On June 14 of 2005 at Toronto, he came full circle.

That year was the first since 2000 without a no-hitter, so Carpenter's one-hit shutout of his former club

Carpenter, who went the distance for the win, is all smiles as he celebrates with catcher Yadier Molina following the Cardinals' 5-0 defeat of the Cincinnati Reds.

Carpenter fires to the plate in the first inning against the Detroit Tigers in Game 3 of the World Series.

Carpenter is congratulated by teammates after pitching a complete game shutout against the Houston Astros.

was arguably the best-pitched game of the year. He needed 95 pitches to get through it, struck out 10 and faced only 28 batters, one more than the minimum.

That game sparked the unmatched run of 16 unbeaten starts, in which Carpenter was 13-0 with a 1.36 ERA. He struck out more batters (115) over those 132 innings than he allowed to reach base (79 hits, 19 walks).

"It was one of those things where you try to anticipate a potential problem," La Russa said. "He was on such a consistent roll already—really, really going at a high level, that you didn't want (Toronto) to be a distraction. He was at 100 percent, and more motivation might tip him over, become a detriment. Then he pitched like that.

"That's when you knew it—you were watching something special."

Carpenter said there are four things a pitcher learns he wants to do in the majors once he arrives: Start opening day, pitch in the All-Star Game, win a Cy Young and win a World Series. He started opening day for the Cardinals, started the All-Star Game for the NL, and won the Cy Young in 2005.

In 2006, he accomplished his fourth goal while compiling a 15-8 record during the regular season, including 221 innings pitched and a 3.09 ERA. He then saved his best performance for the postseason, where he was the dominant pitcher in the playoffs. ■

Carpenter walks off the field after the seventh inning against the Giants. He carried a shutout into the eighth inning for the 100th win of his career.

Old Reliable

Mets' Glavine Shuts Down Cards in Opener

NLCS Game 1 • Mets 2, Cardinals 0

NEW YORK: Sharp and deceptive as ever, Tom Glavine took charge again, putting the pitching-depleted Mets on his 40-year-old back to give New York the lead in the NL championship series.

Carlos Beltran rocked Shea Stadium with a homer that crashed off the scoreboard to back another gem by Glavine, and the Mets beat the St. Louis Cardinals 2-0 in Game 1.

"Tommy was the key," New York manager Willie Randolph said. "He's quiet, goes about his business and is one of the leaders on our staff."

Making his 34th postseason start, Glavine shut down Albert Pujols and extended his scoreless streak to 13 innings in the playoffs.

Beltran, who wore out St. Louis in the NLCS with Houston two years ago, hit a two-run shot off an otherwise impressive Jeff Weaver in the sixth. That was all the offense New York needed to win its eighth straight game, dating to the regular season.

"It pains me," Cardinals manager Tony La Russa said. "No way to suggest that he's a losing pitcher. ...Jeff was outstanding. So was Glavine. We hit too many balls in the air. I mean, it's tough to win when you do that."

After rain postponed the opener, the Cardinals bumped up ace Chris Carpenter, who will pitch on regular rest in Game 2. Rookie right-hander John Maine will be on the mound for the Mets.

Missing injured starters Pedro Martinez and Orlando Hernandez, the Mets are counting heavily on Glavine as they chase their first World Series title in 20 years. The cagey left-hander has delivered in a big way.

He threw six scoreless innings in Game 2 of the first round, helping the Mets to a three-game sweep of the Los Angeles Dodgers. And the two-time Cy Young Award winner, who waited four seasons to reach the playoffs with New York after doing so year after year in Atlanta, was just as good against St. Louis.

"I understand the importance of when I pitch now. But at the same time, I'm trying my best to mentally play games with myself and dismiss that," Glavine said. "I don't want to go out there with any added pressure on myself."

Helped by two inning-ending double plays and a sprawling catch by super sub Endy Chavez, Glavine yielded only four hits and two walks. He struck out Pujols in the first, walked him in the fourth and retired him on a liner to shortstop in the sixth.

Still, the slugger wasn't impressed.

"He wasn't good. He wasn't good at all," Pujols said. "I think we hit the ball hard. We didn't get some breaks."

Guillermo Mota worked a hitless eighth to avoid facing Pujols himself, instead passing the reigning NL MVP along to Billy Wagner. But the Mets' closer got

Jeff Weaver pitched beautifully in Game 1 of the NLCS, but was out-dueled by New York's Tom Glavine.

Pujols to line out to first, and Juan Encarnacion followed with a hard groundout.

Wagner then walked Scott Rolen, who is 1-for-14 this postseason, and retired pinch-hitter Scott Spiezio on a popup for his third save of the playoffs.

Glavine matched Andy Pettitte for the most postseason starts in major league history. Glavine also improved to 14-15 in the postseason, tying Pettitte for the second-most wins behind former Braves teammate John Smoltz (15).

"He made a lot of hitters tonight look foolish, kept them off balance," Mets star David Wright said.

Weaver, cast off by the Los Angeles Angels in July, was nearly as good. He cruised through 5 2-3 innings, blanking the Mets' menacing lineup on one harmless single.

But Paul Lo Duca bounced a hit through the left side in the sixth, and Beltran drove a 2-2 fastball an estimated 430 feet off the giant scoreboard in right-center—the ball clanging off Jose Valentin's No. 18 in New York's lineup.

"Every time you do something in October it means a lot," Beltran said. "Hitting the home run today, of course brings memories."

It also woke up a curiously quiet crowd of 56,311 at Shea, which was plenty noisy during two home games in the division series, and left them chanting "Wea-ver! Wea-ver!"

"I'd been feeding him fastballs all day and he finally caught up to one," Weaver said. "If you would have told me I'd have allowed one hit through five innings, I would have liked our chances. But it just didn't go our way."

The right-hander knows all about tough crowds in New York after an unsuccessful stint with the Yankees from 2002-03, when he was often booed lustily in the Bronx. Weaver, lifted in the sixth after 98 pitches, is scheduled to come back on only three days' rest in Game 5—as is Glavine, who threw 89 pitches.

"There's no question I feel better about coming back on a small pitch count like I had tonight as opposed to getting over 100," Glavine said.

The Cardinals have seen all too much of Beltran in October. He batted .417 with four homers and five RBIs for the Astros in the 2004 NLCS, a series St. Louis won in seven games. Beltran also hit a game-ending homer against the Cardinals in August.

"He's a big-game guy. He's shown what he can do in the postseason," Randolph said. "He has a beautiful swing. He's a very special individual. You don't see the ball jump off the bat like that with many hitters."

La Russa has his team in the NLCS for the third straight season and fifth time in seven years overall—a run that began with a loss to the wild-card Mets in 2000. But St. Louis is 1-3 in its last four NLCS appearances and is still looking for its first World Series championship since 1982.

The winner of Game 1 in the NLCS has reached the World Series 12 of the last 13 years. The 2005 Cardinals were the exception.

The Mets lost left fielder Cliff Floyd early when he aggravated his injured Achilles' tendon while running out a foul fly in the second. After feeling two pops in his foot, he will have an MRI on Friday. He is day-to-day.

Floyd was replaced by Chavez, a defensive whiz, in the top of the third. Chavez got a late break on Ronnie Belliard's fifth-inning looper, but recovered in time to make a diving, snow-cone grab.

Poor baserunning by Pujols cost the Cardinals in the fourth, when he was doubled off first base by Beltran on Encarnacion's soft fly to a center.

"Albert is an outstanding baserunner and I'm not exaggerating," La Russa said. "That was the exception." ∎

Albert Pujols walks back to the dugout after lining out to first base in the Cardinals' Game 1 loss to the Mets.

So Clutch!
Taguchi HR in 9th Stuns Mets, Wagner

NLCS Game 2 • Cardinals 9, Mets 6

NEW YORK: The key hits that will be remembered best from the St. Louis Cardinals' come-from-behind 9-6 victory over the New York Mets in Game 2 of the NLCS are So Taguchi's go-ahead home run off Billy Wagner in the ninth inning and Scott Spiezio's game-tying two-run triple in the seventh.

Perhaps lost in the shuffle was Jim Edmonds' two-run home run in the third. That tied the score at 4 after the Mets jumped on shaky Chris Carpenter.

It was the latest in a long string of clutch hits for Edmonds.

"Jim has a history of rising to the occasion," manager Tony La Russa said. "All you've got to do is just get him healthy enough to play, and that's really the secret."

Edmonds, 36, went a month between starts due to post-concussion syndrome and is taking daily injections to numb a sore left foot. He had 16 homers on July 26, and only three the rest of the season.

Mets pitcher John Maine found out just how dangerous Edmonds still is. Edmonds entered the postseason with 14 extra-base hits in the division series, tied for first on the career list with Chipper Jones, and the homer was his 12th of the postseason.

"Even now, he likes the challenge of hitting behind Albert [Pujols] and he's got a good stroke when he gets

it going," La Russa said.

Carlos Delgado homered twice off an ineffective Carpenter and drove in four runs, sending the Mets to a 6-4 lead after six innings. Jose Reyes doubled, scored twice and added an RBI single for the Mets, who were trying to take a 2-0 lead in the best-of-seven series before it shifts to St. Louis.

Playing in the postseason for the first time in his 14-year career, Delgado hit a three-run shot in the first and a solo drive in the fifth that put New York up 5-4. He was 10-for-21 (.476) in five playoff games with six RBIs, five runs, two doubles and three homers—all to the opposite field.

Chad Bradford replaced starter Maine in the fifth and tossed 1 2-3 scoreless innings as New York manager Willie Randolph turned the game over to his deep bullpen. Left-hander Pedro Feliciano retired pinch-hitter John Rodriguez with a runner on to end the sixth.

Edmonds' two-run shot in the third off a wild Maine tied it at 4. The Cardinals got a two-run double in the second from No. 8 batter Yadier Molina after a key error at first base by Delgado, but Carpenter struggled. When the scheduled series opener was rained out, St. Louis got a chance to bump up its ace and pitch him in Game 2 on regular rest, instead of Game 3.

The 2005 NL Cy Young Award winner didn't look comfortable on the Shea Stadium mound, though,

Jim Edmonds watches his home run sail into the New York night to tie up the second game of the NLCS at 4-4 in the third inning.

Cardinals Rule

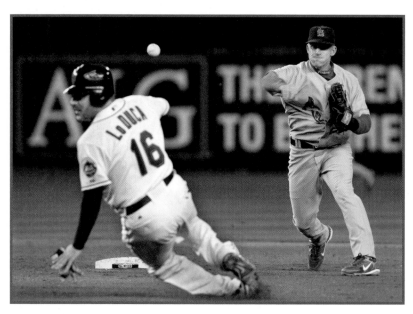

David Eckstein turns two against the Mets during the eighth inning of Game 2 of the NLCS.

unable to find a feel for his curveball on a chilly, 54-degree night.

Reyes led off the bottom of the first with a double to right and advanced on Paul Lo Duca's sacrifice. After Carlos Beltran walked, Delgado drove a 1-1 pitch an estimated 440 feet over the left-center fence for a 3-0 lead. With the boisterous crowd of 56,349 already in a frenzy, Delgado crossed home plate and did a little dance with Reyes.

But two walks by Maine and Delgado's error loaded the bases with none out in the second for St. Louis. Molina, a .216 hitter during the regular season, lined a one-out double over a leaping Delgado for his sixth hit of the playoffs, cutting it to 3-2.

Endy Chavez, starting in left field for New York in place of injured Cliff Floyd, doubled to start the bottom half and moved up on a perfect bunt by Maine. Reyes' single made it 4-2.

The Cardinals also were missing a key player. All-

Star third baseman Scott Rolen, who was 1-for-14 so far in the postseason while struggling with a sore left shoulder, was benched by manager Tony La Russa. Scott Spiezio started at third and batted fifth.

Maine walked Albert Pujols in the third, and Edmonds sent a 2-2 pitch sailing over the center-field fence.

In the rotation because of injuries to Pedro Martinez and Orlando Hernandez, Maine walked five batters in four innings and was lifted for a pinch hitter after 88 pitches. The right-hander gave up four runs—three earned—and two hits, striking out three.

Carpenter, who went 2-0 with a 2.03 ERA in the first round against San Diego, began to settle in after all the early trouble. After Reyes' RBI single, he didn't allow a hit until Delgado's second homer.

Delgado, acquired from Florida in a trade last offseason, became the first Mets player to have a multi-homer game in the postseason since Edgardo Alfonzo in Game 1 of the 1999 division series against Arizona.

Carpenter was pulled for a pinch hitter in the sixth. He yielded five runs, six hits and four walks in five disappointing innings.

The speedy Reyes walked with one out in the sixth and scored easily from first on Lo Duca's double down the left-field line off reliever Josh Hancock, making it 6-4. Before that hit, the St. Louis bullpen, which includes three rookies, had pitched 16 consecutive scoreless innings.

But the Cardinals had the last word about roughing up the bullpen, with Spiezio's game-tying triple in the seventh and Taguchi's game-winning home run of Mets closer Billy Wagner in the ninth. ∎

The St. Louis Cardinals' Incredible 2006 Championship Season

So Taguchi connects for a solo home run off of Mets closer Billy Wagner, breaking a 6-6 tie in the ninth inning en route to a 9-6 Game 2 victory.

Suppan's the Man
Right-hander Dominates Mets for 2-1 Series Lead

NLCS Game 3 • Cardinals 5, Mets 0

ST. LOUIS: During batting practice, scoreboards at Busch Stadium billed Game 3 of the NL championship series as Gotham vs Gateway. With Jeff Suppan doing just about everything for St. Louis, "No contest" would have been much more appropriate.

Suppan hit a rare home run and pitched a tidy masterpiece that gave the St. Louis Cardinals control of the NLCS against the suddenly staggering New York Mets. Scott Spiezio smacked another big triple and St. Louis dazzled on defense, dominating the Mets for a 5-0 victory and a 2-1 lead in the best-of-seven series.

New York lost yet another pitcher to injury when an ineffective Steve Trachsel was clocked by Preston Wilson's comebacker. On offense, the Mets' normally imposing lineup hardly threatened against Suppan, who allowed three hits in eight crisp innings and homered against Trachsel for the second time in two years.

"They say I don't smile in the dugout. I was smiling there, man," Cardinals manager Tony La Russa said. "I thought we got a one-run gift."

With a sea of red-clad Cardinals fans twirling their colorful towels, St. Louis moved within two wins of a trip to the World Series to face the Detroit Tigers, who polished off a four-game sweep of Oakland in the ALCS earlier in the day.

Only 24 hours before, the Mets were in great shape.

After tagging Cardinals ace Chris Carpenter, New York led Game 2 by two runs with two outs and none on in the seventh inning. But the Mets' vaunted bullpen faltered, St. Louis rallied back and the Cardinals grabbed all the momentum with a 9-6 victory.

"I don't think there's any real correlation or carryover from last night to tonight," New York manager Willie Randolph said.

Now the Mets, who cruised to an NL East title and tied the crosstown Yankees for the best regular-season record in baseball, will pin their hopes on erratic lefty Oliver Perez in Game 4.

With a 3-13 record and 6.55 ERA, he'll face Cardinals rookie Anthony Reyes.

"We've been in tougher spots than this," Randolph said. "We feel like we're in pretty good shape, even though we're down 2-1. Things could change real, real quick, so we'll get some rest tonight and I guarantee you we'll be ready to play tomorrow."

But while New York keeps losing key players to injuries, the Cardinals are beginning to get them back. All-Star third baseman Scott Rolen, hampered by a sore left shoulder, returned to the lineup and snapped a 1-for-15 skid with a fifth-inning single. He also made a couple of fine plays in the field.

Trachsel left with a bruised right thigh in the second after getting struck by Wilson's smash, ending a hor-

Scott Spiezio connects for his second two-run triple in as many games against the Mets.

rendous performance in what could have been his final outing with New York.

"It stiffened up pretty quickly and I wasn't able to drive off that leg," Trachsel said.

Already missing Pedro Martinez and Orlando Hernandez, the Mets can't afford another serious injury to a starting pitcher. But if they don't regroup fast, Trachsel's next turn won't come up again anyway.

"He had a little swelling and we'll keep it iced overnight and see how he feels tomorrow," Randolph said. "He seems OK."

The lone positive for New York: long man Darren Oliver chewed up six scoreless innings, saving the rest of the bullpen a bit for Games 4 and 5.

Suppan, who beat Houston's Roger Clemens in Game 7 of the 2004 NLCS, didn't need much help at all. After losing 3-1 to San Diego in Game 3 of the division series, the right-hander struck out four and walked one, throwing 69 of his 99 pitches for strikes in an absolute gem.

"He was so focused and kept making great pitches," La Russa said.

Josh Kinney finished up with a perfect ninth, leaving New York scoreless in its past 12 innings.

With no off day because of a rainout in New York, the Mets and Cardinals had a short turnaround between Games 2 and 3. The Cardinals' charter landed at about 3 a.m. CDT, while the Mets got to their hotel about 4:30 a.m. And New York definitely looked like the tired team in a lethargic performance.

Spiezio sparked St. Louis again with a two-out, two-run triple in the first inning. With Wilson and Albert Pujols aboard, Spiezio hit a drive toward the right-field line that dropped just in front of a diving Shawn Green and deflected away off his chest. Of course, it was Spiezio's two-out, two-run triple (on an 0-2 pitch from Guillermo Mota) off the glove of a leaping Green that tied Game 2 and turned the series.

Leading off the second, Suppan connected on an 0-2 offering and the ball bounced off the top of the left-field fence, just beyond the reach of a leaping Endy Chavez, and into New York's bullpen.

"I don't know. I swung, it ran into my bat," Suppan said.

Suppan's only regular-season homer in 251 career at-bats also came against Trachsel on Sept. 10, 2005. The previous pitcher to homer in the postseason was Kerry Wood for the Chicago Cubs in Game 7 of the 2003 NLCS, off Florida's Mark Redman. Suppan also dropped down two successful sacrifice bunts, drawing chants of "Suuuupe!" from the crowd of 47,053.

Wilson's hard comebacker hit Trachsel on the leg, and the ball ricocheted into shallow left field for a single that put runners at the corners. The right-hander was checked by Randolph and a trainer after hobbling off the mound. Trachsel remained in the game—but not for long. He was removed after a four-pitch walk to Pujols, and Oliver was given as much time as he needed to warm up.

Still, Oliver's second delivery to Jim Edmonds was a run-scoring wild pitch, and Edmonds' RBI groundout made it 5-0. ■

Jeff Suppan worked masterfully against the Mets in Game 3 of the NLCS, putting St. Louis in the proverbial driver's seat.

Power Surge
Beltran's Two HRs Lead Mets Rout

NLCS Game 4 • Mets 12, Cardinals 5

ST. LOUIS: Carlos Beltran sent the ball soaring over the wall. So did David Wright. And Carlos Delgado. And then Beltran did it a second time.

With four home runs, the Mets tied the NL championship series, making sure it will end back home in New York.

"It's all even now. It's, 'Who wants it more?'" Wright said after the Mets battered the St. Louis Cardinals' bullpen in a 12-5 victory that knotted up the series at two games apiece.

Now that Delgado's in the postseason, he's starting to own it. He put New York ahead for good at 5-2 with a three-run homer in the fifth, then busted open the game with a two-run double in a six-run sixth. Beltran boosted his NLCS home-run total to seven in 11 games, Wright broke an 0-for-13 slump with his homer and Jose Valentin added a three-run double in the sixth as New York went ahead 11-3.

"You create you own momentum," Delgado said. "You just have to approach every game like it's the last game you're going to play."

After being held scoreless for 14 innings, the Mets came to life in the third and set a team record for runs and homers in a postseason game. It was more than enough offense to back Oliver Perez, who was forced into the rotation because of injuries to Pedro Martinez and Orlando Hernandez.

New York had 14 hits, one night after getting just three.

"When you have good hitters like we do, you're not going to hold us down too often," Mets manager Willie Randolph said.

But before the series returns to Shea Stadium, Tom Glavine (15-7) is to start for the Mets in Game 5, with Jeff Weaver (5-4) pitching for the Cardinals in a matchup of Game 1 starters. Both would be pitching on three days' rest, though rain is possible. Glavine has pitched 13 scoreless innings in the postseason.

"He knows what it takes, and we're just going to come out tomorrow and play good ball again," Delgado said confidently.

Beltran went 3-for-3 with two walks and is hitting .333 in the NLCS. Delgado is hitting .414 (12-for-29) with four homers and 11 RBIs in the postseason, batting .400 against the Cardinals with three homers and nine RBIs.

"I played 12-and-a-half years and never sniffed the playoffs," he said. "I'm enjoying these playoffs. It's a blast. But I guess it's going to be that much sweeter when you win it."

Perez, acquired July 31 from Pittsburgh along with Roberto Hernandez in the Xavier Nady deal, gave up solo homers to David Eckstein, Jim Edmonds and

Yadier Molina rips an RBI single in the second inning of Game 4 of the NLCS, scoring Scott Rolen for a short-lived Cardinals lead.

Yadier Molina. He never retired the side in order but lasted 5 2-3 innings.

"I did my job, kept us in the game, and that's what's most important," Perez said.

Only the second pitcher to start a postseason game in a year he finished the regular season 10 games under .500 (3-13), Perez had been 0-7 on the road this year.

"We really needed that," Delgado said. "I think he did a fantastic job."

Cardinals rookie Anthony Reyes, who like Perez was pitching for the first time since Oct. 1, allowed runners in all four of his innings, walked four and threw 86 pitches. But he gave up his only runs on the third-inning homers by Beltran and Wright, which put the Mets ahead 2-1.

"I kept the team in the game and tried to do the best I could with every pitch, but I threw too many pitches and I got forced out of there early," Reyes said.

Relievers Brad Thompson and Josh Hancock were lit up for eight runs, with the pair combining to get just one out.

"They are kicking themselves and beating themselves up in the clubhouse," Cardinals manager Tony La Russa said.

Delgado tied the Mets record for RBIs in a postseason series, set by Gary Carter in the 1986 World Series, and set a team record with six extra-base hits. All of his postseason homers have to the opposite field.

"Very, very rare, very unique to see a hitter like him who can turn on you and pull the ball, and then can just stay out there and just serve the ball the other way," Randolph said.

Molina put St. Louis on top in the second with an RBI single and, after the homers by Beltran and Wright, Juan Encarnacion hit a tying triple in the bottom half.

La Russa sent in a pinch hitter for Reyes in the fourth, and Thompson entered in the fifth. Paul Lo Duca reached when second baseman Ronnie Belliard misplayed his leadoff grounder for an error, Beltran singled and Delgado sent an outside 2-0 pitch a few rows into the left-field seats.

"Hopefully this is a one-day thing for us," Thompson said.

Eckstein, who homered just twice in the regular season, connected leading off the bottom half to pull the Cardinals to 5-3. But the Mets loaded the bases with no outs in the sixth against Hancock, and La Russa left him in to face Delgado. Delgado lofted a fly ball to deep left-center that Scott Spiezio took a bad angle on, and the ball bounced over the fence on a hop for a double. A walk to Wright reloaded the bases, Tyler Johnson relieved, and Shawn Green singled to make it 8-3. Valentin then cleared the bases with a double down the left-field line, sending many fans streaming up the aisles.

"It happened quick," Hancock said. "I just didn't do my job. We make mistakes, they hit them."

Perez left after allowing homers to Edmonds and Molina in the bottom half, and Beltran connected for his second solo homer in the seventh, a drive off former-Met Braden Looper. ∎

Rookie hurler Anthony Reyes hangs his head in the dugout after being relieved in Game 4 of the NLCS against the Mets.

Prince Albert

Pujols' Bat, Weaver's Arm Put Cards on Top

NLCS Game 5 • Cardinals 4, Mets 2

ST. LOUIS: One win from the World Series, with their ace on the mound. Albert Pujols and the St. Louis Cardinals are all set to finish off the Mets. A big swing by Pujols and another playoff gem from a rejuvenated Jeff Weaver sent St. Louis to a 4-2 victory over New York and a 3-2 lead in the NL championship series.

Chris Carpenter, last year's Cy Young Award winner, can close it out in Game 6 at Shea Stadium, which would give the Cardinals their second pennant in three years and a date with the Detroit Tigers in the World Series.

"Couldn't ask for a better situation," Weaver said.

Pujols was in a good mood, too, and he actually had a few nice things to say about Tom Glavine this time. After claiming Glavine "wasn't good at all" in the opener even though he pitched seven shutout innings, the 2005 NL MVP finally touched up New York's soft-tossing lefty with a rally-starting homer in the fourth.

"He doesn't give in too much," Pujols said. "I'm just glad it went out of the park."

The Cardinals also got timely hits from Preston Wilson and Ronnie Belliard, and an insurance homer by pinch-hitter Chris Duncan. With the red-clad crowd of 46,496 twirling white towels, St. Louis' young bullpen held on in the late innings after getting roughed up during New York's 12-5 victory in Game 4.

Now, the Mets must count on rookie right-hander John Maine as they try to force a Game 7 at home.

"We're backed into a corner," David Wright said. "We're going to go out there and play relaxed, play loose tomorrow, try to come out swinging and break their hearts."

The second rainout of the series gave Glavine and Weaver a chance to pitch on regular rest instead of only a three-day break. And for the second time in the series, the clubs will travel without a day off. Making his 35th postseason start, the most in major league history, Glavine got just 12 outs.

"They hit my bad pitches. I made a few mistakes tonight and didn't get away with them," he said. "I didn't feel like they made all that many adjustments. I made a mistake to Albert, he hit it. I made a mistake on Preston and he hit it for a double. All the other ones were kind of bloopers and groundballs that went through holes."

Weaver, on the other hand, earned his second impressive playoff victory.

"I think one advantage of playing a team in a long series like this is the opportunity to pitch twice. You get a pretty good read off of their approach last time," Weaver said. "I knew what they had hit before."

Pujols' homer put St. Louis on the board and snapped Glavine's 22-inning scoreless streak that dated to his final regular-season start at Washington.

"I think we made him work," Pujols said. "We hit the

Jeff Weaver pumps his fist after retiring Carlos Delgado to end the fifth inning of Game 5 of the NLCS.

Albert Pujols is congratulated by Scott Rolen after Pujols's solo home run off of New York's Tom Glavine in the fourth inning of Game 5 of the NLCS at Shea Stadium.

ball the other way and he obviously left a couple of balls up. We took advantage."

The 40-year-old Glavine threw four-hit ball in Game 1, beating Weaver 2-0 on Carlos Beltran's two-run homer. But Weaver got the best of this matchup. Cast off by the Los Angeles Angels this summer to make roster room for little brother Jered, the St. Louis right-hander kept Beltran and Carlos Delgado in check, yielding only two runs and six hits in six strong innings.

"I don't even remember the first half of the season," Weaver said. "Just continued to believe in myself that eventually things would turn around."

The Mets put runners at second and third with one out in the eighth, but Randy Flores retired Shawn Green on a shallow fly and rookie Adam Wainwright struck out Jose Valentin looking to preserve a two-run lead. Wainwright fanned Jose Reyes to end the game for his

second save of the postseason.

"He's got so much composure in the toughest situations, so we've gotten a tremendous lift from those guys," St. Louis manager Tony La Russa said.

In this postseason, Cardinals relievers have held opponents to 0-for-31 with two outs and runners in scoring position.

"We didn't have too many opportunities," Mets manager Willie Randolph said. "The bullpen did a great job."

Weaver is 2-1 with a 2.16 ERA in three playoff starts. He tossed five innings of two-hit ball to beat San Diego 2-0 in Game 2 of the first round.

"The biggest key to our win was the way he pitched," La Russa said. "The more you think about what he did, the more credit he deserves."

Valentin's two-run double in the fourth put New York ahead. But while the Mets have scored in 10 innings during the series, seven times St. Louis has responded with at least one run in its next at-bat. Sure enough, Glavine couldn't hold the lead. Pujols pulled a 2-2 pitch barely over the left-field fence in the fourth, his first home run since Game 1 against the Padres and his 12th overall in the postseason.

"Albert just got enough of it, and you get something going," La Russa said. "That got us going and really perked us up."

With two outs, Scott Rolen walked, Jim Edmonds singled and Belliard bounced a tying single through the right side as Delgado broke for first base instead of toward the ball. The Cardinals chased Glavine in the fifth, taking a 3-2 lead on Wilson's RBI double. Duncan, the son of St. Louis pitching coach Dave Duncan, homered off Pedro Feliciano in the sixth.

Glavine threw only 40 of his 80 pitches for strikes, allowing three runs and seven hits in four-plus innings. He also failed to tie former Atlanta teammate John Smoltz for the most wins in postseason history at 15. ■

Albert Pujols celebrates after the final out in the Redbirds' 4-2 win over the Mets in Game 5.

The Maine Event
Rookie Right-hander Tops Carpenter, Forces Game 7

NLCS Game 6 • Mets 4, Cardinals 2

NEW YORK: Even before Game 6, the New York Mets were briefed on travel plans to Detroit for the World Series opener. Brimming with confidence and blocking out adversity, John Maine pitched a game to remember, making sure that itinerary would not be thrown away. And now, the NL championship series comes down to a winner-take-all finale.

The rookie dominated St. Louis with the poise of a veteran, Jose Reyes sparked the offense with a leadoff home run and the Mets rocked 'n' rolled at boisterous Shea Stadium to beat the Cardinals 4-2 and force the NL championship series to a Game 7.

Missing Pedro Martinez and Orlando Hernandez? So what.

With the season on the line, Mets manager Willie Randolph exudes an assured attitude that has filtered down throughout his roster.

"I think if you're going to play the game and you want to be a winner, you have to believe that you can," he said.

Maine outpitched reigning NL Cy Young Award winner Chris Carpenter, escaping a bases-loaded jam in the first and two-on trouble in the third. Maine allowed two hits in the first and none after that, pitching 5 1-3 shutout innings, striking out five and walking four.

"I knew everything was riding on it," he said.

Reyes had three hits and two stolen bases, Shawn Green boosted the lead with a fourth-inning RBI single and Paul Lo Duca let the loud crowd of 56,334 exhale with a two-run, two-out single in the seventh off ex-Met Braden Looper that made it 4-0.

That turned out to be key because Billy Wagner gave up a two-run, two-out double to So Taguchi in the ninth before retiring David Eckstein on a game-ending grounder. Now the pennant comes down to one game and the Cardinals start Jeff Suppan, who won Game 3 with eight scoreless innings.

"This is what you dream," said Cardinals first baseman Albert Pujols, who has just one RBI in the series. "This is what it's all about."

"We'll take our chances with Game 7," the Cardinals' Jim Edmonds said. "We're ready to play."

Maine and Carpenter had crossed paths on their way to New York—both left ahead of their teams to rest up for their starts.

"Maine was on the same flight as me. We got delayed and sat for two hours in St. Louis and ended up not getting here until 11 o'clock," Carpenter said. "He said, 'Hello,' and I said, 'Hello' and that was about it. When we landed it was raining real bad, and we just talked about hoping we didn't get rained out."

There was no rain, and the Shea Stadium crowd was feisty. The volume on the speakers were turned

Pujols points to the heavens after hitting a double off New York's John Maine.

Cardinals Rule

Cardinals players look out from the dugout rail during the seventh inning of Game 6 of the NLCS, won by the Mets to force a Game 7.

Maine, a 25-year-old right-hander obtained in January's dump of Kris Benson to Baltimore, came up with the big outs early, perhaps the biggest of his life. St. Louis had runners at second and third with one out in the first, before Maine fanned Edmonds on three pitches and loaded the bases by hitting Juan Encarnacion. Lo Duca saved a run with a backhand stop of a pitch in the dirt on a 1-2 pitch to Scott Rolen, who then flied out.

"We've got to get at least one there," Cardinals manager Tony La Russa said.

Reyes' home run, a no-doubt-about-it drive to right-center, came when Carpenter left a cutter over the plate on his third pitch. It was Reyes' first in postseason play—his first since Sept. 10.

"As Jose goes, we go," Randolph said. "His energy is infectious."

Eckstein walked leading off the third and stole second, but Maine struck out Scott Spiezio and, after intentionally walking Pujols, retired Edmonds on a fly-out and struck out Encarnacion.

"I think early we could have gotten on him," Spiezio said. "We kind of let him off the hook there, and then he started getting more confidence and started throwing the changeup and the slider for strikes."

That left St. Louis 0-for-5 with runners in scoring position. The Cardinals didn't get another runner past first until the ninth inning. ■

up, and the scoreboard flashed quotes from Mets players praising the fans. In the first Game 6 at the ballpark since the famous comeback against Boston that was capped by Mookie Wilson's grounder through Bill Buckner's legs, the spirit of '86 was invoked on several signs.

"Uno, dos, adios," read another sign.

The Mets even wore their traditional pinstripes, just like in their championship years of 1969 and 1986.

"I looked in the stands a couple of times and it looked like a college students' section. People didn't sit down the whole game," Lo Duca said. "That's an unbelievable feeling. And when something goes your way, it's electric."

So Taguchi smacks a two-run single off Mets closer Billy Wagner in the top of the ninth inning of Game 6 of the NLCS.

A Real Fall Classic
Molina, Suppan Lead Cards into World Series

NLCS Game 7 • Cardinals 3, Mets 1

NEW YORK: The first long drive to left field wound up in the webbing of Endy Chavez's glove as he crashed against the wall. The second one sailed clear over his head. And that's what sent Yadier Molina and the St. Louis Cardinals to the World Series.

Molina's tiebreaking homer in the ninth inning and another Game 7 gem by Jeff Suppan helped St. Louis overcome Chavez's astounding grab, giving the Cardinals a 3-1 victory over the New York Mets on a rainy night for the NL championship.

"I think this is the best team—and we proved it," Molina said.

Adam Wainwright wriggled out of a bases-loaded jam in the bottom of the ninth, striking out St. Louis nemesis Carlos Beltran to end it and leaving a stunned crowd in deflated silence just moments after it had Shea Stadium shaking. With that, the Cardinals earned their second pennant in three years and a date with the Detroit Tigers in Game 1 of the World Series.

Hey Motown, here come the Cards.

"I'm just so happy for Yadier. What a big hit for us," slugger Albert Pujols said.

A .216 hitter with only six home runs during the regular season, Molina drove the first pitch he saw from reliever Aaron Heilman into New York's bullpen for a 3-1 lead in the ninth.

"I just left it up," Heilman said. "I was just trying to throw it down and away. Instead it stayed right over the middle of the plate."

Chavez, who made one of the most memorable catches in postseason history just three innings earlier, could only stand and watch at the fence as the Mets' title hopes were dashed.

"Everybody said I don't hit, and I proved them wrong," said Molina, a standout defensive catcher.

Scott Rolen, robbed of a homer by Chavez in the sixth, started the St. Louis rally with a single. But the Mets, resilient throughout their stirring season, nearly came back in the ninth. Jose Valentin and Chavez singled before pinch-hitter Cliff Floyd struck out looking. Jose Reyes lined to center for the second out, and Paul Lo Duca drew a walk that loaded the bases. That brought up Beltran, who homered three times in the series after hitting .417 with four home runs for Houston in the 2004 NLCS against St. Louis.

Wainwright, a rookie filling in for injured closer Jason Isringhausen, got ahead in the count immediately and froze Beltran with a curveball for strike three.

"I can't let my team down right there," said Wainwright, who has three saves in the postseason. "Our team deserves it. We battled so hard in the playoffs."

The Cardinals, with their 17th pennant in hand,

Yadier Molina, just moments after his tiebreaking home run, celebrates the final out of the Cardinals' epic Game 7 win over the Mets in the NLCS.

New York's Endy Chavez makes a stunning catch to rob Scott Rolen of a two-run home run in the sixth inning of Game 7 of the NLCS, preserving a 1-1 tie.

comes to the plate.

St. Louis stumbled down the stretch and won the NL Central with only 83 wins. Many observers gave them little chance against the Mets, who tied the crosstown Yankees for the best regular-season record in baseball at 97-65.

"I don't think anyone expected, especially late in the season, that the St. Louis Cardinals would be in the World Series," Rolen said.

Suppan, who beat Roger Clemens in Game 7 of the 2004 NLCS, took home the MVP award this time for two outstanding starts. He limited the Mets to one run and five hits in 15 innings, and once again was at his best in a big game. Suppan, who won Game 3, is 106-101 lifetime, but 2-1 with a 1.69 ERA in five NLCS starts. He pitched into the eighth inning and allowed only two hits—none after the first.

"We never gave up. We always believed in ourselves," Suppan said.

The Cardinals, seeking their first World Series title since 1982, ended a long postseason streak by winning Game 7 on the road after dropping Game 6. The previous 11 home teams that won Game 6 of an LCS or World Series to stave off elimination also won Game 7. The last road team to win a seventh game after losing Game 6 was Cincinnati's Big Red Machine at Boston in the 1975 World Series.

Randy Flores worked a scoreless eighth for the win as the Cardinals' young bullpen came through again. Oliver Perez, an unlikely starter for the injury-depleted Mets, matched Suppan most of the night, yielding only one run through six innings. But New York's normally

charged out of the dugout and mobbed Wainwright in front of the mound. During the champagne celebration in their clubhouse, players gathered around several times and chanted "Jo-se, Jose, Jose, Jose," mocking the popular chant Mets fans crow when Reyes

Jeff Suppan confers with Yadier Molina before facing David Wright in the first inning of Game 7.

relentless lineup couldn't muster enough offense.

"It's really disappointing. It was a great game," Mets manager Willie Randolph said. "We just didn't get any big hits."

With a runner on in the sixth, Rolen pulled Perez's first pitch deep to left and Chavez, a defensive whiz starting because Floyd has an injured Achilles' tendon, raced back to the fence as fast as he could. In one motion, the 6-foot Chavez jumped with all his might and reached his right arm up and over the 8-foot wall as far as it would stretch. His mouth wide open, he snagged the drive in the tip-top of his glove—the white of the ball showing atop the webbing like a scoop of vanilla ice cream. Chavez banged into the padded blue wall, buckling a couple of panels, but landed on his feet and came up firing back into the infield.

Jim Edmonds, who had walked, had already rounded second, so second baseman Valentin relayed to first for a spectacular double play that ended the inning with Pujols and the bewildered Cardinals watching from the top step of the dugout in amazement.

"I had to check because my glove almost went out of my hand. I didn't know if I kept it inside," Chavez said. "I jumped as high as I can. Like a 10 percent chance in my mind I could catch it. I had to improvise myself and do it on the run. See the ball, see the wall and do the thing that I've got to do."

Fans chanted "En-dy Cha-vez!" and roared "Whooaaa!" over and over again as the replay was shown several times on the big video board in left-center. Chavez watched, too, and finally came out for a curtain call—a rarity for a defensive play.

Perhaps still thinking about his near-miss but more likely bothered by a slick ball, Rolen, a Gold Glove third baseman, threw away David Wright's slow grounder for a potentially costly error in the bottom of the sixth. That helped the Mets load the bases with one out, but Suppan struck out Valentin. The light-hitting Chavez then had a chance to deliver with his bat, but he flied out, leaving him 0-for-12 with runners in scoring position during the series.

"A little tumultuous inning there for No. 27," Rolen said, referring to himself.

Perez, often leaping over the foul line on his way to the dugout, pitched the game of his life on only three days' rest. This from a guy who was demoted to the minors by lowly Pittsburgh in June and finished 3-13 with a 6.55 ERA this season. In fact, he was barely an afterthought when the Mets acquired him with reliever Roberto Hernandez at the July 31 trade deadline. Perez, however, won Game 4 in St. Louis and gave the Mets all they could have hoped for in Game 7. ■

The Big Chill
Winning Helps Mend Fences for Rolen, La Russa

ST. LOUIS: Cold as it was by the end of Game 3 of the World Series, there seemed to be a thaw between the two glaciers currently sharing the Cardinals clubhouse.

St. Louis manager Tony La Russa and third baseman Scott Rolen haven't talked much since the skipper sat down the slugger in Game 2 of the NLCS because he didn't like the way the perennial all-star was swinging the bat.

Rolen, in turn, didn't like the way he found out about being benched–by looking at the lineup card just hours before the first pitch–and relations between the two have been chillier than the weather ever since.

Winning makes a clubhouse a lot warmer, all by itself, and with a lead in this Series, maybe that helped explain Rolen's good mood after St. Louis clipped the Tigers 5-0 behind a sharp performance from starter Chris Carpenter. Or maybe it had something to do with that small gesture of goodwill La Russa threw his way after Rolen grounded into an inning-ending double play in the bottom of the eighth.

With the bases loaded, Rolen grounded sharply to Detroit's Brandon Inge at third, who stepped on the base and then fired across the diamond to nip Rolen at first. A step past the base, Rolen grabbed his helmet with both hands, wheeled and glared at first-base ump Mike Winters.

"I thought I was safe," Rolen said afterward."Then I went back and looked at the video. I'm an idiot."

La Russa almost certainly knew that, not that Rolen was an idiot, but that he was out at first. Yet he came strolling out of the dugout a second after the call and pleaded the case briefly with Winters.

Though La Russa didn't discuss it afterward, there's a few possible explanations for his actions. The least plausible one is that he expected Winters to change his mind, and since St. Louis was already comfortably ahead by that point, it's not likely he was desperate to get the call overturned. So maybe that little show of support for Rolen was his way of offering an olive branch.

Asked for his take on that gesture, Rolen replied simply, "No idea."

And just before turning to take another question, he smiled.

You won't find two tougher, prouder, more stubborn baseball men than Rolen and La Russa sharing the same town, and St. Louis isn't that big to begin with. The manager was long ago certified as a baseball genius, but since winning it all with the Oakland A's in 1989 and jumping to the Cardinals and the National League in 1996, he's won seven division titles–the last three in a row–but not another Series.

Before this year, he got St. Louis this far only once, and the Cardinals were swept by the Boston Red Sox

Rolen connects for an RBI ground-rule double off San Francisco Giants' Kevin Correia during the seventh inning of a 6-1 win.

Rolen lays out for home as umpire Adam Dowdy watches after hitting a single and benefiting from a three base error by Chicago Cubs' right fielder Jacque Jones.

in 2004. Rolen went 0-for-15 in that one, not long after La Russa, a baseball lifer, called him the best third baseman he'd ever seen and Mike Schmidt, who's arguably one of the best ever at that position, chimed in that Rolen is "better than me."

That's a lot to live up to for anyone. For Rolen, who has played banged-up for so much of his career without complaining, it's been like trying to play with an anvil strapped to his back. When someone asked him about that 2004 Series with a question that began,

"What if?" Rolen cut him off.

"It's better to be good than to suck," he said. "How's that?"

But a moment later, that small smile crossed his lips again and he said, "They can play what-if in that clubhouse on the other side. You can always play what-if."

Considering how hard he is on himself, Rolen needs critics like he needs another broken part. But things surely would have been different in the 2004 postseason if Rolen hadn't rushed back from a calf strain and a bum knee that doctors said was held together by cartilage worn down to the diameter of a shoestring. And they would have been different this time around, too, if Rolen hadn't rushed back from

The strong-armed Rolen fires across the infield in an effort to throw out the Mets' Paul Lo Duca in an August game in New York.

Rolen scores as Chicago Cubs catcher Michael Barrett bobbles the catch and tag attempt in the fifth inning of a game in St. Louis.

The normally reserved Rolen discusses his differences with home plate umpire Tim Tschida during a game against the Houston Astros.

surgery on his left shoulder.

"You get to the spot where you wanted to get your whole life, you hit the ball hard," he said, "and you live with it."

The saving grace is that he's been hitting the ball hard since this Series began. He went 1-for-4 with a walk and scored a run in Game 3, but wasn't interested in any credit.

"Nobody in here is looking at the scoreboard to see who's doing what," he said.

But in the opener, Rolen collected three hits, including a home run, and hit Detroit third baseman Brandon Inge rounding the base to score in a 7-2 victory. La Russa was forced to break his silence that night, "Scott came around like a freight train," the manager said admiringly, and Rolen responded this way:

"It was good for me to kind of turn the page tonight to a new series, a new competition," he said. "I felt like I had a little fight in me tonight."

We don't know for certain whether this is the restart of a lasting friendship, but it's clear that instead of bickering with each other, two very tough guys have temporarily made peace and have no doubts about who the real enemy is. ■

Rolen swings for the fences in an August games against the Cincinnati Reds.

Prime Time

Edmonds Earns His Hollywood Star by Delivering in Clutch

ST. LOUIS: Jim Edmonds' nickname is "Hollywood," a reference to the 36-year-old center-fielder's uncanny knack for coming through when everybody is watching.

St. Louis Cardinals manager Tony La Russa surely had that in mind when he kept putting Edmonds in the lineup against lefties this year, despite a puny .156 batting average against them. Sure enough, facing Detroit Tigers southpaw Nate Robertson in Game 3 of the World Series, Edmonds put his name in lights yet again.

"He's got that quality where the bigger the moment, the more likely he's going to concentrate, not get distracted, and produce," La Russa said. "He's done that ever since he's been here.

"He really is a prime-time guy."

The St. Louis Cardinals' elder statesman, prone more to musing about retirement in a season plagued with injury and struggles at the plate, lined a key double down the first-base line off Robertson in the fourth inning for the first runs in St. Louis' 5-0 victory of Game 3.

"I'm definitely not 25, so I'm just out there having a good time and enjoying the moment," Edmonds said.

Getting to this moment was a long road for Edmonds. Post-concussion syndrome from a collision with a wall kept him out of the lineup for a month. His sore foot requires a daily numbing injection designed to last until the end of the game. And his aching left shoulder will require surgery in the off-season.

So it's far from perfect.

"They've got medication for that and a lot of other things," Edmonds joked. "It's not necessarily pain-free but it's a lot of fun."

Edmonds was so bad against lefties this season that manager Tony La Russa last month discussed the possibility of platooning the four-time all-star and eight-time Gold Glove winner against tough lefties in the playoffs. Then again, La Russa knows Edmonds' history, and he's been out there throughout the post-season, routinely tracking down fly balls even when he couldn't help on offense. In the NL championship series, Edmonds made a spectacular catch at the wall in the sixth inning of Game 5 to rob the Mets' Jose Reyes, a play that didn't make it into the conversation because it came in a 12-5 New York rout.

Edmonds was only 1-for-15 in the 2004 World Series, a rare post-season power outage. But Edmonds' second World Series appearance has been a rousing success.

Edmonds' key double in Game 3 demonstrated that perhaps he just needed time to clear his head. The Tigers were convinced: When Edmonds came to bat again in the seventh with two outs and a runner on third, Jason Grilli walked him intentionally.

"He's obviously swinging the bat real good in the

Edmonds drives in two runs with his bases-loaded double against Tigers pitcher Nate Robertson in the fourth inning of Game 3 of the World Series.

Edmonds belts a two-run home run off Mets pitcher John Maine during the third inning of Game 2 of the NLCS.

post-season," teammate Albert Pujols said. "We need everybody to step up at the right time, and that's what he did."

"Jim has a history of rising to the occasion," La Russa said. "'All you've got to do is just get him healthy enough to play, and that's really the secret."

Coming Back in Style

Edmonds' first at-bat in a month back in September showed he'd lost none of his flair for the dramatic. A night after hitting a three-run pinch homer, Edmonds

was in St. Louis' starting lineup after being side-lined since mid-August due to his post-concussion syndrome.

"That's one thing he's demonstrated," La Russa said. "He'll rise to the occasion."

St. Louis, which had lost six in a row and seen its NL Central lead rapidly shrink, needed some more big moments from Edmonds.

The eight-time Gold Glove center fielder has made a number of acrobatic catches during his seven seasons in St. Louis, and has piled up just as many big hits. Memorably, his extra-inning homer forced Game 7 in the 2004 NLCS, helping propel the team to its first World Series in 17 seasons.

La Russa said Edmonds' clutch production over the

By playing through pain and always hustling, Edmunds is a fan favorite in St. Louis and is a great role model for kids.

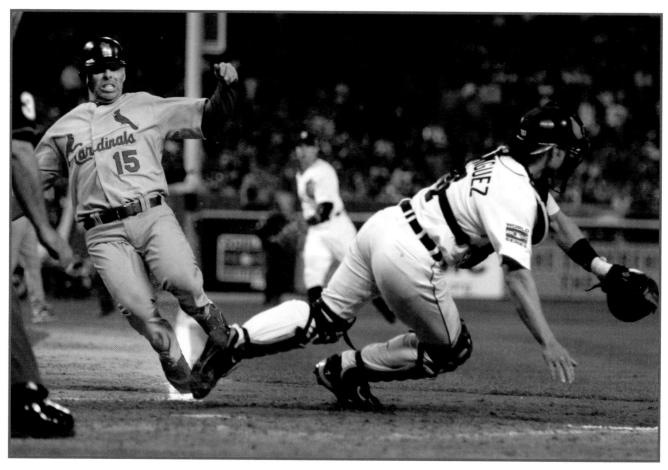

Edmonds slides into home while Tigers catcher Ivan Rodriguez reaches for a wild throw on a fielder's choice by Cardinals' Juan Encarnacion in the sixth inning of Game 1 of the World Series.

years compares favorably with that of teammates Albert Pu-jols and Scott Rolen, Harold Baines from one of his early White Sox teams and Jose Canseco from the Oakland Athletics. He said he's often kidded Edmonds for his ability to come through in a big network game, or if hockey pal Chris Pronger is in attendance.

"Whenever Pronger was around, he'd always show off," La Russa said. "He'd always have a big day. He has that ability to get to that next level."

Edmonds had another of those moments last month with his three-run homer off Mike Thompson that tied it at 5 in the fourth inning, although it wasn't enough to prevent another loss in the team's late-season slide. St. Louis led by the division by seven games on Sept. 20, and led by only 2? entering this particular game.

"It would have been a great story," La Russa said.

Still, neither La Russa nor Edmonds wanted to make too big of a deal of his first meaningful swing in a long time, or his return to the lineup. He was making his first start since August 25, and only his second since August 12, so La Russa said it wouldn't be a total shock if the post-concussion symptoms come back.

Edmonds connects for an RBI single to score Albert Pujols during the fourth inning in Game 2 of the NLDS against the Padres.

Edmonds watches his third inning, two-run homer off New York Mets pitcher John Maine in Game 2 of the NLCS.

La Russa also noted that returning to form after a lengthy layoff is more difficult at age 36.

"Everything is so up in the air," he said. "You just watch and see how he gets through it. He may take two sprints in the outfield and come back and say, 'I'm done.'

"We might as well find out."

Without much conviction, Edmonds said he felt "OK." He told reporters they were making too big a deal of his return.

La Russa eased him in, batting him sixth against former teammate Woody Williams. Edmonds, batting .262 with 19 homers and 68 RBIs in 105 games, had batted fourth or fifth most of the season.

"This is just getting a chance to play, and we'll see how it goes," Edmonds said. "That's all I can say right now. If you go out there and make a fool of yourself and cause the team to lose, then what are we talking about?" ■

Edmonds laughs it off after being forced out at second in an early season game against the Arizona Diamondbacks.

A New Season

Cards Show Postseason Swagger After Stumbling to Finish

NLDS Game 1 • Cardinals 5, Padres 1

San Diego: With one swing of Albert Pujols' bat, a St. Louis Cardinals lineup that looked so sickly in September suddenly got a lot better under the California sun. San Diego Padres ace Jake Peavy tempted Pujols with one pitch too many and the slugger, who has a shot at a second straight National League most valuable player award, responded with a two-run homer that launched the Cardinals to a 5-1 victory in the opening game of the division series.

Everything went well for the Cardinals, from the second chance Pujols got when catcher Mike Piazza couldn't catch his foul ball to having ace Chris Carpenter fresh for the playoff opener, the result of manager Tony La Russa's gamble in keeping him out of the regular-season finale.

Even though they enjoyed home-field advantage for the first time in the opening round, San Diego still can't beat the Cardinals in October. The three-time NL Central champion Cardinals have won seven straight postseason games against the Padres, including division series sweeps last year and in 1996.

The latest win started with Pujols' impressive drive in the fourth inning that broke a scoreless tie. Pujols connected on Peavy's eighth pitch.

"What an at-bat," St. Louis leadoff hitter David Eckstein said. "Being able to foul off pitches, take some pitches and then do what he did, that ignited the whole club."

Peavy was hoping for far better results than Game 1 of last year's playoff series, when he lost 8-5 to Carpenter at St. Louis while pitching with two broken ribs. Peavy hurt himself when he jumped on Trevor Hoffman's head while celebrating the Padres' division title several days earlier.

Pujols, though, reminded Peavy and the Padres just how dangerous of a hitter he is. Peavy left a full-count cut fastball over the plate and Pujols drove it an estimated 422 feet into the Padres' bullpen beyond the fence in left-center. Center fielder Mike Cameron climbed halfway up the fence in a futile effort at Pujols' 11th career postseason homer, which hushed the sellout crowd of 43,107 at Petco Park. Chris Duncan was aboard on a leadoff single.

Peavy and manager Bruce Bochy had talked about letting the situation dictate whether they pitched to Pujols, or put him on.

"I don't think about if they're going to pitch to me because I want to be aggressive," Pujols said. "If I start thinking a lot of things like that, that's going to take my aggression away. I just take whatever they give me, you know. And if they give me a good pitch today, I'm going to try to put my best swing and hopefully help my team out to win."

Cardinals shortstop David Eckstein is congratulated by teammates after scoring on Jim Edmonds' RBI single in the fifth inning.

Peavy knew he had little margin for error.

"It was a cutter that was right down the middle," Peavy said. "Yeah, those go wrong a lot."

The at-bat was kept alive when Piazza got a late jump on Pujols' foul pop and couldn't catch it at the screen. Pujols thought the ball was heading for the stands. Piazza couldn't tell if the ball hit the screen on the way down, but added: "I felt like I should have made the play. I really don't have an excuse. It's just one of those things that when you get a situation like that, we need a break to get an out like that."

Following Pujols' homer, Jim Edmonds singled, Scott Rolen doubled and Juan Encarnacion hit a sacrifice fly.

Pujols hit a three-run homer off Padres rookie reliever Cla Meredith in a recent 4-2 win at St. Louis that may have saved the Cardinals' season. St. Louis lost nine of its last 12 regular-season games. Overall, the two-time NL West champion Padres have lost eight straight postseason games dating to 1998, when they were swept in the World Series by the New York Yankees.

While Peavy struggled—he left to a mixture of boos and light applause in the sixth—Carpenter, the reigning NL Cy Young winner, kept the Padres' suspect offense off-balance with his curveball, limiting San Diego to one run and five hits in 6 1-3 innings. He struck out seven and walked one.

Carpenter was pitching for the first time since losing 7-5 to the Padres at St. Louis a week earlier. La Russa gambled and held Carpenter out of the regular-season finale in case the right-hander would have been needed Monday in the makeup of a rainout against the Giants. But that became moot when Atlanta beat Houston, giving the Cards the NL Central title.

"If there's a way of pitching him today, our club plays better when he pitches," La Russa said. "Nobody in the league is better than he is."

Carpenter made adjustments and got out of jams.

"My stuff was good," he said. "My location was good. And my breaking ball was very good."

The Padres came into this series more confident and healthier than the Cardinals, who backed into the playoffs after barely avoiding one of the worst September collapses ever. But, said Padres leadoff hitter Dave Roberts, "Those guys have a lot of confidence when it comes to the postseason. They've had a lot of success. Today was definitely evidence."

Down 5-0, San Diego finally broke through against Carpenter in the sixth. Roberts legged out a one-out triple to the left-center gap, his third hit, and scored on Brian Giles' sacrifice fly. The Padres had two big scoring chances and came away empty, including loading the bases with one out in the seventh, when they chased Carpenter but couldn't score. Second baseman Ronnie Belliard made a sensational diving stop of Todd Walker's grounder and threw him out to end the seventh.

Carpenter also got out of a jam in the fourth after allowing two singles opening the inning.

Edmonds hit an RBI single for the Cardinals in the fifth and Yadier Molina's RBI base hit in the sixth gave St. Louis a 5-0 lead and chased Peavy. Peavy allowed five runs 11 hits in 5 1-3 innings, struck out two and walked one. ∎

Chris Carpenter delivers a pitch in the first inning against the Padres, en route to a 5-1 victory in Game 1 of the NLDS.

Dream-Weaver

Rejuvenated Righty Mows Down Padres

NLDS Game 2 • Cardinals 2, Padres 0

SAN DIEGO: Getting out of September intact was the hard part for the St. Louis Cardinals, who clinched a division title while stuck in reverse. And the San Diego Padres? Well, after coming into the playoffs with all the confidence in the world—and rare home-field advantage—they may not make it through the weekend.

The Padres appear to be headed for their same ol' postseason fate against the Cardinals, who won 2-0 behind Albert Pujols and reclamation project Jeff Weaver to take a 2-0 lead in the NL division series.

"It's very big because coming into these playoffs we didn't really know what to expect," Cardinals shortstop David Eckstein said.

Well, history suggests the best-of-five series will end in St. Louis, unless the popgun Padres can find their missing bats. The Padres are hitting an embarrassing .164 in the series, getting just 10 hits and one run so far, while striking out 20 times. They're 0-for-10 with runners in scoring position, and have stranded 13.

The crowd booed after Cardinals rookie closer Adam Wainright retired the side in the ninth.

"We've got to get on the board, score some runs," said San Diego native David Wells, who may have pitched his final big league game. "I think one run in two games isn't going to cut it. This continues, then you know that's the end of it.

"Right now, I mean it's about as flat as it can get," said the 43-year-old Wells, who plans to retire when the season ends.

St. Louis, which barely avoided one of the biggest

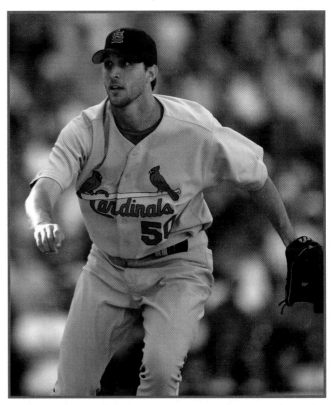

Cardinals closer Adam Wainwright goes after a ground ball in the final inning of St. Louis's 2-0 victory over the Padres.

Cardinals pitcher Jeff Weaver delivers in the first inning of Game 2 of the NLDS. Weaver shut the Padres down en route to a 2-0 victory and a 2-0 series lead.

Albert Pujols drives in a run in the fourth inning of the Cardinals' 2-0 win over San Diego in Game 2 of the NLDS.

September collapses ever, improved to 8-0 in the postseason against San Diego. That includes division series sweeps last year and in 1996.

"I think it's a huge step in the right direction to come into somebody else's park and win the first two, especially in the short series," said Weaver, who used his curveball to baffle a lefty-dominated Padres lineup. "We're looking forward to getting back home and trying to make the series as short as possible."

Pujols had three more hits after homering in the 5-1 victory in Game 1. He and Jim Edmonds hit RBI singles off Wells in the fourth inning.

Weaver and four relievers, three of whom are rookies, combined on a four-hitter. Making his second career postseason start, Weaver outpitched Wells, who was making his 17th postseason start and 27th appearance dating to 1989.

Weaver gave up two singles in five innings, allowing only two Padres baserunners as far as second base. He struck out three and walked three.

Aware that the Padres liked fastballs, Weaver didn't throw very many. San Diego leadoff batter Dave Roberts estimated that more than 50 percent of Weaver's pitches were curveballs.

"I just wanted to stay away from the extra-base hits and things of that nature, and was able to throw a lot of quality breaking balls to keep these guys off-balance," said Weaver, who dodged jams in the first and fifth.

And to think Weaver struggled so badly with the Angels this year, going 3-10, that he was traded to make room in their rotation for his younger brother, Jered. But he earned this start by going 4-1 with a 4.03 ERA in eight road starts with St. Louis.

Relievers Randy Flores, Josh Kinney, Tyler Johnson and Wainwright pitched four innings of two-hit ball. Wainwright got the last four outs.

Padres rookie Josh Barfield doubled off Wainwright with two outs in the eighth before Adrian Gonzalez grounded to second.

So why have San Diego's bats gone AWOL?

"It's one of those things where we struggle at home offensively," Brian Giles said. "There's no sugarcoating it. I wish we had an explanation. We don't."

About the only thing the Padres have going now is that they were 45-36 on the road, including winning two of three at St. Louis last week.

"We battled our tails off through September to get here," said Geoff Blum, who filled in for injured shortstop Khalil Greene. "Hopefully, there are some remnants of that floating around and we'll return to some of the magic in St. Louis." ■

The Padres' Josh Bard literally goes down swinging against Jeff Weaver in the sixth inning of Game 2.

Off the Schneid

Padres Finally Get One Off Cards

NLDS Game 3 • Padres 3, Cardinals 1

St. Louis: Russell Branyan, Chris Young and Trevor Hoffman saved San Diego, stopping the St. Louis Cardinals from sweeping the Padres in the first round of the NL playoffs.

Branyan's two-run double in the fourth gave the NL West champions their first lead in three games, Young shut down the Cardinals' offense for 6 2-3 innings and Hoffman made it to the mound for the first time in the series in a 3-1 victory that pulled the Padres to 2-1 in the best-of-five playoff.

St. Louis, which swept San Diego in the first round last season while never trailing, sends ace Chris Carpenter to the mound in Game 4, when the Padres will try to force the series back to San Diego for a fifth game.

"I think Chris is as good as anybody in baseball," Cardinals manager Tony La Russa said. "So I always think we have a chance, a good chance. It's a game we hoped not to play."

Woody Williams, who lost Game 3 last year, will start for the Padres. Game 1 loser Jake Peavy would go in Game 5.

"Probably as much as having confidence in Woody, we think Jake could use another day," manager Bruce Bochy said. "He's pitched a lot down the stretch, and we're in a situation where we need to win two games."

Carpenter will be made his third straight start against the Padres, including his final regular-season outing.

"No matter what game it is and how many times you've seen them, the goal is to execute pitches and execute your game plan," Carpenter said. "If you can do that you'll have success. If you don't, you won't."

San Diego was 1-for-14 with runners in scoring position in the series before Branyan's hit off loser Jeff Suppan put the Padres ahead 2-0. Geoff Blum followed with a sacrifice fly.

Young, a 6-foot-10 right-hander, was the NL's best road starter, going 6-0 with a 2.41 ERA. Making his first postseason appearance, the 27-year-old allowed four hits, walked two and struck out nine, fanning Albert Pujols and Scott Rolen twice each. He is 9-0 in 24 road outings dating to June 25, 2005.

Alan Embree finished the seventh, Scott Linebrink allowed an eighth-inning homer to pinch-hitter So Taguchi and Hoffman finished the five-hitter with a perfect ninth for his fourth postseason save.

Padres manager Bochy had been 0-8 against the Cardinals in the playoffs, with his team also getting swept in 1996.

"No getting away from it, they've had their way with us," Bochy said. "We're hearing 'Who's your Padre?' There's a real sense of relief to finally win a game against these guys in the playoffs. It took a

Cardinals manager Tony La Russa watches the closing moments of Game 3 of the NLDS.

Padres closer Trevor Hoffman is congratulated by Geoff Blum after saving game 3 of the NLDS to close to within 2-1 of the Cardinals.

well-pitched game."

Hoffman led the NL with 46 saves this season and set the career record with 482, passing Lee Smith. He pitched only one inning in last year's series against St. Louis.

San Diego won despite stranding 14 and going 1-for-15 with runners in scoring position, leaving the Padres at 1-for-25 in the series. San Diego scored one run in losing the first two games at home.

Pujols, who had five hits in the first two games, was 0-for-4 with two strikeouts and a double-play grounder. The second strikeout came with runners on first and second for the second out in the sixth, and

Jim Edmonds followed with a flyout to the wall in left.

Suppan escaped a second-and-third, no-outs jam in the first when Brian Giles hit a comebacker, Dave Roberts hit into a forceout at the plate and catcher Yadier Molina picked off Mike Piazza at first.

San Diego went ahead when Adrian Gonzalez singled with one out in the fifth, Mike Cameron walked and Branyan drove the ball into the right-field corner. Branyan took third on the throw, with second baseman Ronnie Belliard leaping and then stumbling to retrieve the off-line relay from right fielder Juan Encarnacion, and scored on Blum's fly.

Taguchi, who homered only twice in 316 at-bats during the regular season, homered leading off the eighth and Chris Duncan walked with one out. But with the crowd of 46,634 chanting "M-V-P!" Pujols grounded into a double play. ■

Albert Pujols heads back to the dugout after one of two strikeouts in Game 3 of the NLDS.

Redemption
Cards Shift Momentum to Advance to NLCS

NLDS Game 4 • Cardinals 6, Padres 2

ST. LOUIS: Standing on a folding chair in a raucous clubhouse, Albert Pujols sprayed champagne in every direction. Teammates got soaked—even owners—no one was immune.

The tension from Chris Carpenter's shaky beginning, the angst of the St. Louis Cardinals' late-season swoon, all had evaporated. They're going to the NL championship series for the third straight season.

"From Day 1, I kept saying this team's got what it takes to get to the World Series," Scott Spiezio said. "We're a step closer."

Carpenter recovered from a bad first inning to gain his second victory of the series, Juan Encarnacion hit a tiebreaking triple and the Cardinals beat the San Diego Padres 6-2 to win their best-of-five first-round NL playoff 3-1.

St. Louis nearly wasted a seven-game lead in the final two weeks of the regular season but rebounded against the Padres, a team the Cardinals swept in the first round in 2005.

Escaping trouble in each of the last two innings, the Cardinals sealed the win when Adam Wainwright got Dave Roberts on a groundout with two on. Pujols stepped on the first-base bag for the final out to set off the first postseason celebration at the new Busch Stadium, which opened this year.

"I didn't blame anybody who didn't think we had a very good shot," said Cardinals manager Tony La Russa, who improved to 20-5 in the division series. "I'm so pleased because it's been such a rough year. We've popped champagne twice, and the goal is to pop it four times."

Back in the NLCS for the third straight year, the Cardinals open the next round at the New York Mets, who won the season series from St. Louis 4-2.

"They've got a great club," Carpenter said. "We're going to celebrate tonight and worry about them tomorrow."

While the Cardinals won the NL pennant in 2004 before getting swept by Boston, the Cardinals lost last year's NL championship to Houston in six games.

San Diego manager Bruce Bochy, whose team won the division for the second straight year, dropped to 1-9 in the postseason against the Cardinals, who also swept the Padres in the opening round in 1996. San Diego was 2-for-32 (.063) with runners in scoring position in the series.

"This was a pretty good year," Bochy said. "Sure, it's disappointing the way it ended. We didn't score a lot of runs in the series, and that was the difference."

Carpenter, who won the opener 5-1, fell behind 2-0 in the first inning when he walked Russell Branyan with the bases loaded and Mike Cameron followed

The Cardinals celebrate their Game 4 victory over the Padres, sending them to the NLCS for the third straight year.

two pitches later with an RBI grounder.

"I think he was a little bit too pumped up in the first inning," Pujols said.

But that was all the NL West champions would get off Carpenter. He got Josh Barfield to hit into an inning-ending forceout.

"We did have a good chance there to break the game open," Bochy said. "We just didn't deliver."

Carpenter followed with six innings of shutout, five-hit ball, leaving him at 2-0 with a 2.02 ERA in the series and 4-0 with a 2.10 ERA in five postseason starts. La Russa was especially pleased that Carpenter prevented San Diego from building a big lead in the first.

"That was classic Chris, because at the end of the inning they had two runs and not four or five," La Russa said. "Then he started pounding the strike zone."

Because La Russa pitched him instead of saving him for a possible fifth game, he likely won't be available until the third game of the NLCS. San Diego held back ace Jake Peavy for a possible Game 5, which would have been Monday in San Diego. Woody Williams, who took the loss, allowed four runs and five hits in 5 1-3 innings.

He quickly gave back the lead. Ronnie Belliard, 6-for-13 in the series, tied it in the bottom half of the first with a two-run, two-out single. The score stayed tied until the four-run sixth. Pujols started off the bottom half with a five-pitch walk and, one out later, Encarnacion drove a hanging breaking ball deep to right as Pujols lumbered around the bases for a 3-2 lead.

"I left a curveball up," Williams said. "I guess he was looking to go the other way."

Cla Meredith relieved and hit Belliard with a pitch, and Spiezio singled up the middle on a 1-2 pitch to score Encarnacion. Yadier Molina's sharp single to right loaded the bases, and Carpenter hit a grounder to Branyan. The third baseman's throw was wide to

the first-base side and pulled catcher Josh Bard off the plate as Belliard slid home for a three-run lead.

"It was just a tough play," Branyan said. "I went hard to my left to get to the ball, and I thought I had to rush the throw home, and my momentum was carrying me toward first, and I pulled the ball—I pulled it off line."

On the very next pitch, David Eckstein bunted up the first-base line, sending Spiezio home on the squeeze.

San Diego, in the playoffs in consecutive years for the first time, put runners at the corners with no outs in the eighth on singles by Brian Giles and Adrian Gonzalez. Tyler Johnson relieved and struck out Bard. Mike Piazza, who didn't start after banging up his shoulder in San Diego's 3-1 Game 3 win, then pinch hit. Josh Kinney came in to pitch and got Piazza to bounce into an inning-ending 6-4-3 double play.

The St. Louis bullpen, featuring three rookies, threw 13 1-3 scoreless innings in the series.

"We didn't know much about these guys," Roberts said. "They've got great stuff. To their credit, they made pitches when they had to." ∎

Chris Carpenter is congratulated by teammate Scott Rolen after being pulled in the eighth inning of Game 4 of the NLDS against the Padres.

Focus Pocus
Suppan Steps Up When Cards Need a Lift

NEW YORK: Trouble was mounting due to circumstances beyond Jeff Suppan's control. So the St. Louis Cardinals' pitcher did what he always does, focused on the next pitch.

Suppan ignored a raucous road crowd anticipating a big inning, blocked out the steady rain and concentrated on the task. His sixth-inning escape from a bases-loaded jam in the Cardinals' 3-1 victory gave him another Game 7 to remember and the NLCS MVP award.

"That was probably the moment," manager Tony La Russa said. "The crowd is flying, the team is flying high."

Suppan never looks back. La Russa admires that dogged approach.

"He goes start to start the same way, hitter to hitter the same way," the manager said. "It's really a great way to go when you're playing in pressure situations."

Suppan is just another guy in the regular season, with a career 106-101 record. In the postseason, he stands out.

In 2004 he outpitched Roger Clemens to help the Cardinals make it to the World Series for the first time in 17 years. His Game 7 effort against the Mets—seven-plus innings, two hits, one run—kept it close until Yadier Molina's two-run home run in the ninth sent the St. Louis back once again.

Suppan succeeded after ace Chris Carpenter fell short in St. Louis' first shot at finishing off the Mets in Game 6. Carpenter is considered to be the team's best pitcher by far, but won neither of his NLCS starts.

Suppan also threw eight shutout innings and hit his second career home run in Game 3, a 5-0 victory, to give the Cardinals the series lead.

"He finally gets what he deserves," Carpenter said. "He's done it a long time for us and pitched in a lot of big games for us, and he deserves everything he gets."

Suppan is 2-1 with a 1.69 ERA in five NLCS starts. He also pitched the clincher in the division round against the in 2004, and supplied goggles for the pitching staff so they could avoid the champagne sting.

If Suppan was the stand-in ace in the NLCS, Wainwright was just as effective filling in for injured closer Jason Isringhausen. The ninth inning of Game 7 even had an edge-of-your-seats Isringhausen feel, with the Mets loading the bases before Wainwright froze Carlos Beltran on a curveball for the final out.

"When I got him 0-2, I said, 'You know what, I'm going to make one more good pitch,' " Wainwright said. "One more great pitch and let's go to the Series."

Wainwright, a key prospect acquired in a trade with the Braves for J.D. Drew in 2003, has been projected as a starter next season. He's 3-for-3 in save chances in the postseason, allowing no runs in 6 2-3 innings.

The gritty Jeff Suppan delivers a strike in the first inning of a game against the San Diego Padres.

Suppan makes like a first baseman as he scoops the ball out of the dirt in a game against the Cubs.

Suppan's story is more an unlikely tale of dominance. He was 13 games below .500 for his career before signing a free-agent deal with the Cardinals in 2004. The previous year he was left off the Red Sox's division-series roster and wasn't used in the ALCS.

In Game 7 this year, Suppan saved his best pitching for the toughest spot.

It was 1-1 in the sixth when third baseman Scott Rolen's throwing error let the Mets load the bases with one out. Suppan struck out Jose Valentin and got Endy Chavez—who had robbed Rolen of a two-run home run with a leaping catch the top half of the inning—on a lazy fly ball to center.

"All you can do is the best you can," Suppan said.

"You're really able to go out there pitch by pitch, and that's what I did.

"I just tried to keep rolling and forget about what happened in the past."

The Cardinals advanced despite finishing the NLCS in a 1-for-21 slump with runners in scoring position. They scored their other run on two singles and Ronnie Belliard's safety squeeze bunt off Oliver Perez in the second.

The Gamer

David Eckstein, the shortstop with the infectious go-go attitude, the "pulse" of the St. Louis Cardinals, needed a tuneup. Worn down by injuries since June, he now has a sprained left shoulder, courtesy of a diving stop on Jose Reyes' infield hit during Game 5 of the NL championship series.

Suppan bears down in a game against the Florida Marlins in late August.

Suppan scores from first on a double to center field by Cards' David Eckstein in a game against the Pirates.

Since then, he has taken fewer batting practice cuts than his teammates and has avoided unnecessary throws to conserve his strength for games. He skipped a recent off day at Busch Stadium while the rest of his teammates went through a mandatory workout. Eckstein's defense hasn't been affected, though he has had no success at the plate in the World Series or much in the postseason overall.

"I limit my swings in the on-deck circle, limit batting practice," Eckstein said. "If the other guys are taking three sessions in the cage, I'll take one or two.

"I limit all the stuff I do before the game."

Eckstein, who batted .292 in the regular season, is 0-for-9 against the Tigers with a strikeout and a double-play ball to end the eighth inning in the Cardinals' 3-1 loss in Game 2. He was hitting .160 overall (8-for-50) in the postseason with two extra-base hits, a homer and a double, and two RBIs, until he disproved all unbelievers with a Series Game 4 performance of four hits and two RBIs, including the game-winner.

Trainer Barry Weinberg said the latest injury isn't so severe that Eckstein wouldn't have tried to play through it during the regular season. Weinberg also noted the heart factor.

"Is he 100 percent? No. Is he playable? Yeah," Weinberg said. "So he plays. That's David, that's his nature. He pushes on and he doesn't want to not be

Pirates catcher Humberto Cota waits for the late relay throw from right field as the hard-charging David Eckstein scores on a sixth-inning single.

Eckstein demonstrates his solid defense by getting to this ground ball in a game against the Cubs.

in the lineup."

Teammate Scott Rolen said Eckstein deserves to be out there, if he thinks he can play.

"If he gives the nod that he can go out and play, he earned it and we want him out there," Rolen said. "I believe the man. I'll take him out there any day."

Pitcher Chris Carpenter called Eckstein "a leader in this clubhouse."

"He's a leader on the field and he comes every day to play the game as hard as he can," Carpenter said. "He's a big part of this club."

In the postseason, it's common for players to soldier through aches and pains accumulated from six months of competition.

"Man, there's a lot of people banged up right now," Preston Wilson said. "That's part of the game, that's part of what you do.

"Playing banged up right now is better than sitting at home."

Those have always been words to live by for Eckstein, although this year he was limited to 123 games, sidelined with a concussion and later a side injury.

The Cardinals have a capable backup in Aaron Miles, who did a nice job filling in during Eckstein's side injury. It's highly unlikely, though, that Eckstein will ask for time off.

Unfortunately, he's been banged up," Weinberg said. "He plays so hard a lot of times it catches up with him.

"But you can't tell him to back off his game, because that's not who he is." ■

David Eckstein avoids the take-out attempt by the Milwaukee Brewers' David Bell.

All is Fair...

La Russa and Leyland's Friendship an Afterthought During Series

DETROIT: Jim Leyland woke up at 4:15 a.m. one day during the AL championship series in Oakland, called his kids back East and wished his son a happy birthday.

Then, since he was up, he called one of his best friends—Tony La Russa.

"We chatted for a little while and I went back to bed," Leyland said.

Now, the Detroit Tigers manager wants to put to rest a really good baseball story: his longtime friendship with LaRussa, the St. Louis manager who is playing quite a different role in Leyland's life these days.

Their teams will play against each other as the World Series gets under way.

"I'm going to say this at the beginning of the World Series and hopefully end it. I'm not going to talk about Tony La Russa and myself this series at all," Leyland said sternly the day before Game 1. "I know some Cardinal players and have the utmost respect for everybody, obviously including Tony, but I'm not going to make that a story during the World Series because I don't think that should be a story."

This story should be about the players. And that's what it's going to be about from my end."

Like a good friend, La Russa was on the same page.

"When the series is over, we'll reflect," he said. "Right now, we're not going to get into the personal stuff. Everybody knows we're friends."

Leyland and La Russa have been close for decades. After Leyland was passed over by the Tigers to be their manager—or a coach on Sparky Anderson's staff—La Russa gave him his first job in the majors as third-base coach for the Chicago White Sox in 1982.

Three seasons later, Leyland's ascent as one of this era's great managers began in Pittsburgh, where he led the Pirates to three straight division titles and won two NL manager of the year awards.

Leyland went on to win a World Series with the Florida Marlins in 1997, then exited the dugout as a burned-out manager in Colorado two years later.

That's when La Russa was there for his friend—again—helping him land a gig as a Pittsburgh-based scout for the Cardinals before he resurfaced in Detroit this season. Leyland said it was the best six years of his life.

"The Cardinals treated me like gold, they just didn't pay me much gold," Leyland joked.

La Russa and Leyland often talk on the phone after games—win or lose—and the latest chat came morning after St. Louis outlasted the New York Mets in Game 7 of the NL championship series.

The friendly chats will fade out, La Russa insisted.

"I'll guarantee you, starting tomorrow we won't talk very much over the next 10 days," he said.

Whoever wins will join Anderson, who won titles in

La Russa embraces his close friend and Tigers skipper Jim Leyland before the start of Game 1 of the World Series.

La Russa argues with second base umpire Steve Rippley during NLCS against the Mets.

Detroit and Cincinnati, as the only managers in baseball history to win the World Series in both leagues.

"I have a regret about it a little bit only because it's such a significant accomplishment and Sparky is such a significant part of our lives," La Russa said. "You kind of wish he could have it by himself."

In his fifth World Series—a total that trails just seven managers—La Russa has a chance to add to the championship he won in 1989 with the Oakland Athletics and move further out of Whitey Herzog's shadow.

After leading St. Louis to the 2004 World Series, its first in 17 years, La Russa signed a new contract that keeps him with the storied organization through 2007.

"I know Jim Leyland respects and loves Tony La Russa for not just the way that he manages, but the person he is," Tigers pitcher Nate Robertson said. "It's probably like going up against your brother."

Dirty Politics

In the aftermath of Game 2 of the World Series, La Russa kept talking about Kenny Rogers, his words from the interview room booming all around Busch Stadium, courtesy of the PA system. One by one, the Detroit Tigers stopped their workout to listen.

"I don't believe it was dirt," they heard the St. Louis manager say. "Didn't look like dirt."

A lot of baseball fans weren't buying Rogers' explanation, either. So instead of looking to Game 3 of the World Series, the focus stayed squarely on Game 2.

The wily La Russa is considered one of the best minds in baseball today.

Cardinals hold out their palms with a mark on their hands in reference to Kenny Rogers before Game 3 of the World Series.

Specifically, on what Rogers had at the base of his left thumb—and whether it was there before.

"We know it's all over the place right now," umpires' supervisor Steve Palermo said.

Some photographs from Rogers' start in the AL championship series against Oakland showed what appeared to be the same kind of smudge on his pitching hand that caught everyone's attention.

Prompted by La Russa, the umpires asked Rogers to clean off his left hand before the second inning. He wound up pitching eight shutout innings in a 3-1 vic-

tory that evened the World Series at one game each.

Rogers, who's gone from playoff farce to post-season force this October, insisted it was an innocent mistake.

"I rub up the balls between the innings and before the game all of the time," Rogers said. "I rub up the bullpen balls I pitch with with mud, resin, spit. I do it all the time. They rub the ball up, too, with mud before the games.

"The game balls, they're dirty. Usually, when I get done, there's not much on my hand, but I guess a little bit more than normal. I wiped it off and proceeded to pitch seven pretty good innings," he said. "Mud, resin, sweat. It's always there. I try not to go crazy with it, but it's not making my pitches do anything crazy."

Later, it was La Russa's turn to have his say. His off-

Tigers pitcher Kenny Rogers made as much noise with the brown substance on his left hand as he did with his pitching in Game 3 of the World Series.

day news conference was piped over the Busch Stadium public-address system, so his thoughts echoed from every corner of the empty ballpark. The Tigers had just come onto the field for practice, and they were instantly surrounded by La Russa's voice giving a lengthy analysis.

The first question skipped right past Game 3, with reigning NL Cy Young winner Chris Carpenter starting against Nate Robertson. Instead, it was about Rogers, who has pitched 23 scoreless innings this post-season—after going 0-3 with an 8.85 ERA in previous post-seasons.

La Russa's answer went on for five minutes. He said he brought the smudge to the umpires' attention, but did not demand they search Rogers. They didn't. La Russa also said the Cardinals were aware Rogers had a similar spot earlier in the post-season.

"I said, 'I don't like this stuff, let's get it fixed.' If it gets fixed let's play the game. It got fixed, in my opinion," he said.

"If he didn't get rid of it, I would have challenged it. But I do think it's a little bit part of the game at times, and don't go crazy," he said.

La Russa also said he talked to the Cardinals before they worked out.

"I briefly explained where I was coming from and I said, 'Anybody felt like I should do different, then I disappointed you.' ... And they didn't raise their hand and say, 'Hey, I disagree,' they just didn't say anything," he said. "But it's very possible there were guys that disagreed. It's not the way we want to win."

La Russa also was adamant that his longtime friendship with Leyland did not affect how he handled the situation.

"It had nothing to do with Leyland," he said.

Palermo said he talked with plate umpire Alfonzo Marquez about how to best settle the flap, advising that a quick word with Rogers would work. That satisfied La Russa.

"Tony did things in a good and professional manner to resolve the issue," Palermo said.

Umpires can inspect a pitcher on their own if they believe something is wrong. A manager can ask an umpire to check, too.

In 2002, the Cleveland Indians suspected Rogers was scuffing balls and asked the plate umpire to search for anything illegal. Nothing was found. Pitchers occasionally will put substances on their hands to help grip the ball in cold weather. Tigers reliever Todd Jones once wrote a newspaper column admitting he'd used pine tar—that's illegal—when he pitched at Colorado.

"I'm saying in my particular case, in situations like that, I have in the past done that," he said. "Guys are not scuffing and guys are not using Vaseline. That's a vast difference than a guy who can't feel anything and is using something to get a grip."

This episode has become perhaps the most-discussed Series smudge since Game 5 in 1969, when Mets manager Gil Hodges brought umpire Lou DiMuro a ball with shoe polish to persuade him that Cleon Jones had been hit by a pitch from Baltimore's Dave McNally.

Asked about the flap, Leyland brushed it aside.

"I'm not going to chew yesterday's breakfast and I'm not going to comment on it," he said.

Baseball's vice president of umpiring, Mike Port, said Randy Marsh's crew took a "pro-active" stance to diffuse the dirty issue. Rogers is scheduled to pitch in Game 6, if the Series returns to Comerica Park.

"Certainly things carry forth and create a certain vigilance," Port said.

Said Palermo: "Obviously, it's going to be a thing that everyone talks about. And we'll be well aware of it if there is a next time." ■

La Russa exchanges views with second base umpire Angel Hernandez after LaRussa disagreed with his call in a game against the Padres.

Season Recap

APRIL

Gm	Date	Team Opp		Score	W-L	Time	Winner	Loser
1	Mon, Apr 3	STL @PHI	W	13-5	1-0	2:54	C Carpenter	J Lieber
2	Wed, Apr 5	STL @PHI	W	4-3	2-0	2:52	B Thompson	T Gordon
3	Thu, Apr 6	STL @PHI	W	4-2	3-0	3:09	J Marquis	C Lidle
4	Fri, Apr 7	STL @CHC	L	1-5	3-1	2:13	G Maddux	J Suppan
5	Sat, Apr 8	STL @CHC	L	2-3	3-2	2:35	B Howry	B Thompson
6	Sun, Apr 9	STL @CHC	L	4-8	3-3	2:57	S Williamson	J Isringhausen
7	Mon, Apr 10	STL MIL	W	6-4	4-3	2:42	M Mulder	T Ohka
8	Wed, Apr 12	STL MIL	W	8-3	5-3	2:26	J Marquis	D Bush
9	Thu, Apr 13	STL MIL	L	3-4 (11)	5-4	3:41	J de la Rosa	J Isringhausen
10	Fri, Apr 14	STL CIN	L	0-1	5-5	2:43	A Harang	C Carpenter
11	Sat, Apr 15	STL CIN	W	9-3	6-5	2:29	S Ponson	D Williams
12	Sun, Apr 16	STL CIN	W	8-7	7-5	3:04	B Looper	Weathers
13	Mon, Apr 17	STL @PIT	W	2-1	8-5	2:18	J Marquis	P Maholm
14	Tue, Apr 18	STL @PIT	L	4-12	8-6	2:46	O Perez	J Suppan
15	Wed, Apr 19	STL @PIT	W	4-0	9-6	2:12	C Carpenter	V Santos
16	Fri, Apr 21	STL CHC	W	9-3	10-6	2:29	M Mulder	J Williams
17	Sat, Apr 22	STL CHC	W	4-1	11-6	2:54	S Ponson	G Rusch
18	Sun, Apr 23	STL CHC	L	3-7	11-7	2:22	G Maddux	J Marquis
19	Mon, Apr 24	STL PIT	W	7-2	12-7	2:25	C Carpenter	O Perez
20	Tue, Apr 25	STL PIT	W	6-3	13-7	2:39	J Suppan	V Santos
21	Wed, Apr 26	STL PIT	W	4-3	14-7	2:32	J Isringhausen	R Hernandez
22	Thu, Apr 27	STL WSN	W	6-2	15-7	2:46	S Ponson	M O'Connor
23	Fri, Apr 28	STL WSN	L	3-8	15-8	2:51	T Armas	J Marquis
24	Sat, Apr 29	STL WSN	W	2-1	16-8	2:22	B Looper	J Rauch
25	Sun, Apr 30	STL WSN	W	9-2	17-8	2:51	J Suppan	Z Day

Season Recap

MAY

Gm	Date	Team Opp		Score	W-L	Time	Winner	Loser
26	Mon, May 1	STL @CIN	L	1-6	17-9	2:20	B Arroyo	M Mulder
27	Tue, May 2	STL @CIN	L	2-3	17-10	2:35	T Coffey	B Falkenborg
28	Wed, May 3	STL @HOU	L	4-5	17-11	2:54	R Oswalt	J Marquis
29	Thu, May 4	STL @HOU	L	3-4	17-12	2:46	A Pettitte	C Carpenter
30	Fri, May 5	STL @FLA	W	7-2	18-12	2:47	J Suppan	S Mitre
31	Sat, May 6	STL @FLA	W	7-6	19-12	3:12	M Mulder	D Willis
32	Sun, May 7	STL @FLA	W	9-1	20-12	3:09	J Hancock	S Olsen
33	Mon, May 8	STL COL	L	2-6	20-13	2:35	J Francis	J Marquis
34	Tue, May 9	STL COL	W	4-2	21-13	2:26	A Wainwright	J Mesa
35	Wed, May 10	STL COL	W	7-4	22-13	3:01	J Suppan	B Kim
36	Fri, May 12	STL ARI	W	5-3	23-13	2:41	M Mulder	J Cruz
37	Sat, May 13	STL ARI	W	9-1	24-13	2:48	J Marquis	C Vargas
38	Sun, May 14	STL ARI	L	6-7	24-14	3:07	L Vizcaino	A Wainwright
39	Tue, May 16	STL NYM	L	3-8	24-15	3:07	T Glavine	J Suppan
40	Wed, May 17	STL NYM	W	1-0	25-15	2:32	M Mulder	S Trachsel
41	Thu, May 18	STL NYM	W	6-3	26-15	2:41	J Marquis	J Lima
42	Fri, May 19	STL @KCR	W	9-6	27-15	2:46	C Carpenter	M Redman
43	Sat, May 20	STL @KCR	W	4-2	28-15	2:56	A Reyes	D Bautista
44	Sun, May 21	STL @KCR	W	10-3	29-15	2:54	J Suppan	S Elarton
45	Mon, May 22	STL @SFG	L	2-9	29-16	2:51	J Wright	M Mulder
46	Tue, May 23	STL @SFG	W	8-5	30-16	2:36	J Marquis	M Morris
47	Wed, May 24	STL @SFG	W	10-4	31-16	2:51	A Wainwright	N Lowry
48	Fri, May 26	STL @SDP	L	1-7	31-17	2:37	C Hensley	J Suppan
49	Sat, May 27	STL @SDP	W	4-3	32-17	2:41	S Ponson	C Park
50	Sun, May 28	STL @SDP	L	8-10	32-18	2:59	J Peavy	M Mulder
51	Mon, May 29	STL HOU	W	3-1	33-18	2:46	J Marquis	T Miller
52	Tue, May 30	STL HOU	L	3-6	33-19	2:35	A Pettitte	J Hancock
53	Wed, May 31	STL HOU	W	4-3 (11)	34-19	3:42	B Looper	M Gallo

Season Recap

JUNE

Gm	Date	Team Opp		Score	W-L	Time	Winner	Loser
54	Fri, Jun 2	STL CHC	L	4-5 (14)	34-20	5:04	R Dempster	J Hancock
55	Sat, Jun 3	STL CHC	L	5-8	34-21	2:43	G Rusch	M Mulder
56	Sun, Jun 4	STL CHC	W	9-6	35-21	3:00	J Marquis	G Maddux
57	Mon, Jun 5	STL CIN	L	7-8	35-22	3:10	E Yan	J Isringhausen
58	Tue, Jun 6	STL CIN	L	0-7	35-23	2:42	E Milton	C Carpenter
59	Wed, Jun 7	STL CIN	L	4-7	35-24	2:49	A Harang	S Ponson
60	Fri, Jun 9	STL @MIL	W	10-6	36-24	3:35	J Hancock	J Winkelsas
61	Sat, Jun 10	STL @MIL	L	3-4	36-25	3:09	M Wise	R Flores
62	Sun, Jun 11	STL @MIL	W	7-5	37-25	2:59	J Hancock	D Bush
63	Tue, Jun 13	STL @PIT	W	2-1	38-25	2:22	C Carpenter	O Perez
64	Wed, Jun 14	STL @PIT	L	7-9	38-26	2:50	Z Duke	S Ponson
65	Thu, Jun 15	STL @PIT	W	6-5	39-26	3:19	M Mulder	V Santos
66	Fri, Jun 16	STL COL	W	8-1	40-26	2:25	J Marquis	A Cook
67	Sat, Jun 17	STL COL	W	6-5	41-26	2:38	J Suppan	J Francis
68	Sun, Jun 18	STL COL	W	4-1	42-26	2:28	C Carpenter	J Fogg
69	Tue, Jun 20	STL @CHW	L	6-20	42-27	3:23 J	Vazquez	M Mulder
70	Wed, Jun 21	STL @CHW	L	5-13	42-28	2:20	M Buehrle	J Marquis
71	Thu, Jun 22	STL @CHW	L	0-1	42-29	2:00	F Garcia	A Reyes
72	Fri, Jun 23	STL @DET	L	6-10	42-30	2:42	J Verlander	C Carpenter
73	Sat, Jun 24	STL @DET	L	6-7 (10)	42-31	3:42	J Zumaya	T Johnson
74	Sun, Jun 25	STL @DET	L	1-4	42-32	2:31	W Ledezma	S Ponson
75	Mon, Jun 26	STL CLE	L	3-10	42-33	2:58	C Lee	J Marquis
76	Tue, Jun 27	STL CLE	L	1-3	42-34	2:41	C Sabathia	A Reyes
77	Wed, Jun 28	STL CLE	W	5-4	43-34	3:06	J Isringhausen	B Wickman
78	Fri, Jun 30	STL KCR	L	5-7 (10)	43-35	3:40	A Burgos	B Looper

Season Recap

JULY

Gm	Date	Team Opp		Score	W-L	Time	Winner	Loser
79	Sat, Jul 1	STL KCR	L	7-8 (11)	43-36	4:03	L Hudson	J Isringhausen
80	Sun, Jul 2	STL KCR	W	9-7	44-36	2:59	J Marquis	M Wood
81	Mon, Jul 3	STL @ATL	L	3-6	44-37	2:28	J Smoltz	A Reyes
82	Tue, Jul 4	STL @ATL	W	6-3	45-37	2:43	C Carpenter	J Thomson
83	Wed, Jul 5	STL @ATL	L	4-14	45-38	2:52	C James	J Suppan
84	Thu, Jul 6	STL @HOU	L	2-4	45-39	2:54	T Buchholz	S Ponson
85	Fri, Jul 7	STL @HOU	W	8-2	46-39	2:46	J Marquis	W Rodriguez
86	Sat, Jul 8	STL @HOU	W	7-6 (10)	47-39	3:18	J Isringhausen	R Oswalt
87	Sun, Jul 9	STL @HOU	W	7-5 (12)	48-39	3:53	B Looper	B Lidge
88	Thu, Jul 13	STL LAD	W	3-2 (14)	49-39	4:21	B Looper	O Perez
89	Fri, Jul 14	STL LAD	W	5-0	50-39	2:08 C	Carpenter	D Lowe
90	Sat, Jul 15	STL LAD	W	2-1 (10)	51-39	3:09	B Looper	D Baez
91	Sun, Jul 16	STL LAD	W	11-3	52-39	2:49	A Reyes	B Penny
92	Mon, Jul 17	STL ATL	L	3-15	52-40	3:12	H Ramirez	J Weaver
93	Tue, Jul 18	STL ATL	L	5-14	52-41	2:49	T Hudson	J Marquis
94	Wed, Jul 19	STL ATL	W	8-3	53-41	2:32	C Carpenter	J Shiell
95	Fri, Jul 21	STL @LAD	W	2-0	54-41	2:51	J Suppan	B Penny
96	Sat, Jul 22	STL @LAD	W	6-1	55-41	2:42	J Weaver	A Sele
97	Sun, Jul 23	STL @LAD	W	6-1	56-41	2:45	J Marquis	C Billingsley
98	Mon, Jul 24	STL @COL	L	0-7	56-42	2:16	J Francis	A Reyes
99	Tue, Jul 25	STL @COL	W	1-0	57-42	2:30	C Carpenter	J Jennings
100	Wed, Jul 26	STL @COL	W	6-1	58-42	2:56	J Suppan	A Cook
101	Thu, Jul 27	STL @CHC	L	4-5	58-43	3:25	R Novoa	T Johnson
102	Fri, Jul 28	STL @CHC	L	5-6	58-44	3:01	C Marmol	J Marquis
103	Sat, Jul 29	STL @CHC	L	2-4	58-45	2:53	G Maddux	A Reyes
104	Sun, Jul 30	STL @CHC	L	3-6	58-46	3:06	C Zambrano	C Carpenter

Season Recap

AUGUST

Gm	Date	Team Opp		Score	W-L	Time	Winner	Loser
105	Tue, Aug 1	STL PHI	L	3-5	58-47	3:01	S Mathieson	J Suppan
106	Wed, Aug 2	STL PHI	L	8-16	58-48	3:35	B Myers	J Weaver
107	Thu, Aug 3	STL PHI	L	1-8	58-49	3:00	C Hamels	J Marquis
108	Fri, Aug 4	STL MIL	L	3-4	58-50	2:49	D Davis	C Carpenter
109	Sat, Aug 5	STL MIL	W	4-3	59-50	2:55	A Reyes	B Sheets
110	Sun, Aug 6	STL MIL	W	7-1	60-50	2:33	J Suppan	C Capuano
111	Mon, Aug 7	STL @CIN	W	13-1	61-50	2:56	J Weaver	E Ramirez
112	Tue, Aug 8	STL @CIN	L	3-10	61-51	3:10	E Milton	J Marquis
113	Wed, Aug 9	STL @CIN	L	7-8	61-52	2:56	R Franklin	J Isringhausen
114	Thu, Aug 10	STL @CIN	W	6-1	62-52	2:58	A Reyes	B Arroyo
115	Fri, Aug 11	STL @PIT	L	1-7	62-53	2:18	Z Duke	J Suppan
116	Sat, Aug 12	STL @PIT	L	2-3	62-54	2:35	I Snell	J Weaver
117	Sun, Aug 13	STL @PIT	L	0-7	62-55	2:55	P Maholm	J Marquis
118	Tue, Aug 15	STL CIN	W	5-0	63-55	2:30	C Carpenter	A Harang
119	Wed, Aug 16	STL CIN	L	2-7	63-56	2:49	B Arroyo	A Reyes
120	Thu, Aug 17	STL CIN	W	2-1	64-56	2:17	J Isringhausen	R Franklin
121	Fri, Aug 18	STL @CHC	W	11-3	65-56	2:52	J Marquis	C Marmol
122	Sat, Aug 19	STL @CHC	L	4-5 (10)	65-57	3:35	M Wuertz	J Isringhausen
123	Sun, Aug 20	STL @CHC	W	5-3	66-57	2:14	C Carpenter	J Mateo
124	Tue, Aug 22	STL @NYM	L	7-8	66-58	2:36	A Heilman	J Isringhausen
125	Wed, Aug 23	STL @NYM	L	8-10	66-59	3:21	S Trachsel	M Mulder
126	Thu, Aug 24	STL @NYM	L	2-6	66-60	2:34	D Williams	J Marquis
127	Fri, Aug 25	STL CHC	W	2-0	67-60	2:47	J Suppan	J Mateo
128	Sat, Aug 26	STL CHC	W	2-1	68-60	2:23	R Flores	R Novoa
129	Sun, Aug 27	STL CHC	W	10-6	69-60	3:14	B Looper	B Howry
130	Tue, Aug 29	STL FLA	L	1-9	69-61	2:42	S Olsen	M Mulder
131	Wed, Aug 30	STL FLA	W	13-6	70-61	3:26	J Marquis	R Nolasco
132	Thu, Aug 31	STL FLA	W	5-2	71-61	3:07	B Looper	S Mitre

Season Recap

SEPTEMBER

Gm	Date	Team Opp		Score	W-L	Time	Winner	Loser
133	Fri, Sep 1	STL PIT	W	3-1	72-61	1:54	C Carpenter	Z Duke
134	Sat, Sep 2	STL PIT	L	0-1	72-62	2:36	M Capps	J Weaver
135	Sun, Sep 3	STL PIT	W	6-3	73-62	2:38	A Reyes	I Snell
136	Mon, Sep 4	STL @WSN	L	1-4	73-63	2:10	R Ortiz	J Marquis
137	Tue, Sep 5	STL @WSN	W	2-0	74-63	2:40	J Suppan	P Astacio
138	Wed, Sep 6	STL @WSN	L	6-7	74-64	3:10	C Cordero	J Isringhausen
139	Thu, Sep 7	STL @ARI	W	6-2	75-64	2:50	J Weaver	M Batista
140	Fri, Sep 8	STL @ARI	L	1-13	75-65	2:24	L Hernandez	A Reyes
141	Sat, Sep 9	STL @ARI	L	0-3	75-66	1:54	B Webb	J Marquis
142	Sun, Sep 10	STL @ARI	L	7-9	75-67	3:13	L Vizcaino	J Sosa
143	Mon, Sep 11	STL HOU	W	7-0	76-67	2:29	C Carpenter	T Buchholz
144	Tue, Sep 12	STL HOU	W	6-5	77-67	3:03	B Looper	B Lidge
145	Wed, Sep 13	STL HOU	L	1-5	77-68	2:57	R Oswalt	J Marquis
146	Fri, Sep 15	STL SFG	W	14-4	78-68	2:48	J Suppan	B Hennessey
147	Sat, Sep 16	STL SFG	W	6-1	79-68	2:27	C Carpenter	M Morris
148	Mon, Sep 18	STL @MIL	L	3-4	79-69	3:09	F Cordero	B Looper
149	Tue, Sep 19	STL @MIL	W	12-2	80-69	2:52	J Weaver	B Sheets
150	Wed, Sep 20	STL @MIL	L	0-1	80-70	2:33	F Cordero	T Johnson
151	Thu, Sep 21	STL @HOU	L	5-6	80-71	2:17	D Borkowski	C Carpenter
152	Fri, Sep 22	STL @HOU	L	5-6	80-72	3:08	C Qualls	B Looper
153	Sat, Sep 23	STL @HOU	L	4-7	80-73	3:02	D Wheeler	T Johnson
154	Sun, Sep 24	STL @HOU	L	3-7	80-74	3:09	C Qualls	J Hancock
155	Mon, Sep 25	STL SDP	L	5-6	80-75	3:03	S Cassidy	B Thompson
156	Tue, Sep 26	STL SDP	L	5-7	80-76	3:02	W Williams	C Carpenter
157	Wed, Sep 27	STL SDP	W	4-2	81-76	2:48	T Johnson	S Linebrink
158	Thu, Sep 28	STL MIL	L	4-9	81-77	3:25	D Davis	J Marquis
159	Fri, Sep 29	STL MIL	W	10-5	82-77	2:56	J Weaver	C Capuano
160	Sat, Sep 30	STL MIL	W	3-2	83-77	2:46	T Johnson	B Shouse
161	Sun, Oct 1	STL MIL	L	3-5	83-78	2:23	C Villanueva	A Reyes
162	Canceled							

TRIUMPH
BOOKS